Fascinating
book of a complex
author who from young
age touched the world with
his words and so they still
go forward... h 2·2018

Kipling

Jad Adams

Kipling

First published in Great Britain in 2005 by
Haus Publishing Ltd
70 Cadogan Place
London SW1X 9AH
www.hauspublishing.com

This revised edition published in 2012

Copyright © Jad Adams, 2005, 2012

Cover image courtesy Album/Prisma/akg

The moral right of the author has been asserted

A CIP catalogue record for this book is available from the British Library

ISBN 978-1-908323-06-4

Typeset in Berkeley by MacGuru Ltd

Printed in India by HT Media Ltd., Noida

Contents

Introduction

*I*t does not much matter what people think of a man after his death, wrote Kipling near the end of his life, with a scornful eye on future biographers.[1]

With a view to frustrating biography, he set about the destruction of many of his own papers, and those of his parents, and wrote an autobiography almost comically deficient in its description of his life events.

He knew his life would attract interest. He was the most famous English writer in the days when Britain ruled the largest empire ever known; he was the first writer of English to win the Nobel Prize.

His work was richly biographical: Kipling was cruelly abandoned and abused as a child, but was to create some of the most enduring children's characters ever written in Mowgli and Kim.

He took inspiration for his children's tales from his own children but, to his despair, two were to die young. Family quarrels and the mental illness of those around him cursed his middle years; and in old age simplistic political views, crudely expressed, diminished his reputation.

He has been castigated as a misogynist, though few writers of either sex have written so warmly about middle-aged women. Similarly, he can be criticised for his racial views, but no other artist wrote with such intimacy of native life. He was physically unfit for military service but his identification with soldiers was so deep that real soldiers started acting like the characters in his stories.

Kipling was in London in the spectacular 1890s, placing him in the spectrum of literary 'decadents' and 'hearties', when it was by no means obvious in which group he fitted. The contradictions in his character are revealed in his biographical novel *The Light that Failed*, which gives an insight into the challenge of the New Woman to society, the paralysing confusion which struck men when presented by a woman who, like the woman Kipling himself loved, had her own goals in life, her own work and her own sexual self-sufficiency.

Kipling was the first world writer, making his home in four continents. While he is thought of as quintessentially Indian, he in fact spent only 12 of his 70 years in India, visiting the country for the last time at the age of 25. He married an American and spent the first four years of his married life in the United States. He kept a home in South Africa for 35 years, to the end of his life. America supplied his wife, the formidable Carrie; and Africa a father-figure for his mature years in the form of Cecil Rhodes. He had a close relationship to France all his life, which was reciprocated in the acclaim he received there.

Kipling's work is now so well known that many people who have never read any Kipling think they have. He added more phrases to the language than any writer except Shakespeare and the translators of the King James Bible.

Unlike his contemporaries in London – Conan

Doyle, Oscar Wilde or Bram Stoker, who created one enduring character each – Kipling created a cast of characters who live independently of the stories, such as Mowgli, Mrs Hauksbee, Kim and Mulvaney. The only recent writer he resembles in this is Dickens, another immensely prolific writer and also a journalist as well as a fiction writer. In verse, Kipling is a true successor to Browning, Swinburne and Tennyson, whose clear influences he shows. His poem 'If' is still among the best known in the English language.

Despite his many achievements, Kipling was always a subject of controversy: at first he was adored by reviewers; after 1891 he was attacked by the critics yet adored by the public; as the 20th century wore on he fell from favour with the public but increasingly began to enjoy the grudging respect of critics. Regardless of the criticism, this multi-faceted man will not go away: his work stays in print and new generations around the world read him. As George Orwell said, 'During five literary generations every enlightened person has despised him, and at the end of that time nine tenths of those enlightened persons are forgotten and Kipling is in some sense still there'.[2] He wrote thus in 1942, a truth which is undiminished by the passing years.

A Poor White

With his rich evocation of the Indian sub-continent, it is difficult to imagine Rudyard Kipling as anything but a son of India, though his birth in Bombay in 1865 was largely a matter of chance. The Kipling family had arrived in India less by design or desire than as a result of a successful job application.

Kipling's father, John Lockwood Kipling, the son of a Methodist minister, became an architectural sculptor, securing a post at the Department of Science and Art in South Kensington. On departmental trips to the potteries in Staffordshire he became friendly with the family of another Methodist minister, Frederick Macdonald, who had five lively sisters. John Lockwood (always known by his middle name) first met Alice Macdonald at a picnic at Lake Rudyard, Staffordshire, in spring 1863. She was pretty and witty, and they discovered a common love of Browning and other artistic interests.

The Macdonald sisters were to weave themselves deeply into the fabric of artistic and political life in England, giving Rudyard Kipling a network of contacts which belied the impression he often sought to give of a struggling writer who had achieved everything by his own efforts. He was in fact born into a highly successful and influential family. His aunt Georgina married the leading Pre-Raphaelite painter Edward Burne-Jones; his aunt Agnes married another successful artist, Edward Poynter; his aunt Louisa married a wealthy iron-master, later chairman of the Great Western Railway and father of Stanley Baldwin the prime minister.

By comparison Alice's marriage to Lockwood Kipling on 18 March 1865 in Kensington was not felt to be a great match, though the reception was a grand affair attended by such luminaries as Swinburne, Rossetti and Ford Madox Brown.

Lockwood, eager to make his way in the world, had accepted a post as architectural sculptor at the School of Art and Industry in Bombay. The newlyweds sailed on 12 April 1865, and Rudyard was almost certainly conceived on the journey. They arrived at Bombay, the Gateway of India, which was rapidly becoming the commercial heart of the sub-continent. With neither having any previous family experience of India, Alice and Lockwood Kipling must have experienced what would later be called culture shock when they first encountered the heat, the crowds, smells, sounds and colours of India when the ship docked to be met by teeming crowds of porters, hawkers and families waiting for the boat, amid a crush of rickshaws, carriages and working animals, including elephants.

Lockwood took up his position at the school of art founded by a Parsee, Sir Jamsetjee Jeejeebhoy. He wanted Bombay to become an artistic as it was an industrial centre, rather as English industrialists in Manchester and Birmingham had turned from the mere production of wealth to the cultivation of the arts. Lockwood set to work learning Indian techniques and materials and reviving the great Indian art of sculpture.

Alice Kipling settled down to pregnancy in unfamiliar surroundings in a whitewashed bungalow close to the Jeejeebhoy School of Art, which was still under construction. She had to learn how to deal with the servants, who were far more numerous than in households she had known in England, and to come to terms with the rigid Anglo-Indian social hierarchy in which the Kiplings occupied a far from senior position.

The birth of her son was difficult, taking six days; a labour relieved, the servants said, only when they sacrificed a goat kid to the goddess Kali. The baby arrived on 30 December 1865 and was christened Joseph Rudyard Kipling, though he was always known as Rud or Ruddy.

The British India into which Kipling was born in 1865 was just seven years old, having been founded in 1858 by the India Act. The British had progressively dominated India, with a series of spectacular military victories, the most notable of which was Clive's at Plassey in 1757. The country was governed, however, by the East India Company, the primary objective of which was obviously commercial.

In 1857 the behaviour of the company with its indifference to native culture and religious concerns led to the armed rebellion of Indian troops referred to as the Indian Mutiny (many Indians now think of it as the First War of Independence). After the suppression of the Mutiny, the British government's response to the conditions which had brought it about was the India Act, making the India Office in London responsible for rule with the cabinet post of Secretary of State for India and the appointment of a Viceroy of India. Queen Victoria was to be declared Empress of India in 1877.

When Alice Kipling became pregnant again, in 1867, the family decided to return to England to have the baby and she set sail with her rumbustious two-year-old. Her sisters had many fine qualities but they were not excessively maternal and they found their nephew with his loud cries of 'Ruddy is coming!' an irritant.[3] A sister to Kipling was born on 11 June 1868, after another difficult labour, and was christened Alice, though she was always known by her father's name for her, Trix. A third child was born and died in India in 1870, and the Kiplings must have decided that given Alice's poor health and the problems of previous births, they would be content with two children.

Back in Bombay, Kipling – Rud-baba to the doting servants – learned to speak Hindustani as naturally as English, or even more so, and had to be corrected when he used the vernacular in his parents' drawing room. Kipling later wrote of how he *spoke 'English', haltingly translated out of the vernacular idiom that one thought and dreamed in. He delighted in the far going Arab dhows on the pearly waters, and gaily dressed Parsees wading out to worship the sunset.*[4] Kipling had been born into a Methodist family but christened in the Church of England; his sister's Goan Roman Catholic nurse took him to her church; and his Hindu bearer, Meera, took him to Shiva's temple. Rudyard was to make little, if any, distinction between God as manifest in these different traditions, and was when writing his memoirs to ascribe all his good fortune to *Allah the Dispenser of Events*.[5]

The parents and two children left India in April 1871 for a visit to England when Rudyard was five. After an unremarkable round of family visits they stayed at lodgings. Their parents then took the children one morning to a house in Southsea and left them there; and returned to India. Their children were boarded with strangers they had found in a newspaper advertisement. They had said goodbye to Rudyard who was just short of his sixth birthday; Trix, at two, was too young to understand. His parents told him at dawn he must learn quickly to read and write so they might send him letters and books, and left him in a house *smelling of aridity and emptiness*.[6] Why the children were not placed with their aunts is a mystery. Perhaps the subject had been broached and the aunts were not receptive; perhaps Lockwood and Alice, the poor relations, forbore to ask such a favour and preferred to rely on their own meagre resources. They would not bring up their children in India from terror that they would 'go native' and become culturally more Indian than English. One of Kipling's finest works, *Kim*, is the story of precisely such an Anglo-Indian child who grows up owing more to the bazaars and temples than the tea parties.

The woman with whom they lodged made a living by taking in children whose parents were in India. Sarah Holloway was hewn of coarse material which was not softened by marriage to her social superior, a former naval man described as a sea-captain, who was much older than her. The captain was kindly to Rudyard and enjoyed taking him to see the boats at Portsmouth, but it was Mrs Holloway who was the dominant figure in

Kipling's life. As Kipling wrote, the establishment was *run with the full vigour of the Evangelical as revealed to the Woman. I had never heard of Hell, so I was introduced to it in all its terrors.*[7] He called it The House of Desolation.

The children speculated miserably on why they had been abandoned, unable to understand what had led their parents to leave them to such horrors. Mrs Holloway told them it was because they had been naughty and she had taken them in out of pity. Her husband explained that it was because India was too hot for children, which they found hard to credit as Kipling had been there for five years with no ill effect. The Holloways' son Harry told them they were workhouse brats who had been taken in out of charity and nothing of theirs really belonged to them. He broke Trix's doll to prove it.

Transgressions such as spilling a drop of gravy at dinner, forgetting to put a slate away or 'crying like silly babies' when they were read letters from their parents in Bombay led to the punishment of separation from each other and solitary confinement for 24 hours.

Kipling, who could not yet read, was made to do so *without explanation, under the usual fear of punishment.* One day he realised reading was not an obligation but a joy, the opening of the door on a magical world, *a means to everything that would make me happy.*[8] He was soon reading adventure stories from all corners of the Empire; he was later to acknowledge the influence of these works on his own writing.

As soon as his pleasure was known, deprivation from reading was added to the list of punishments. Mrs Holloway was suspicious of his imaginative activities and ordered him to play in a way that she could hear. Kipling rigged up a construction of child's bricks and a little table and would work the table to provide the necessary banging noises of playing while he got on with reading a book. Inevitably he was found out, and punished for *acting a lie*.[9]

Horrifyingly for the child Kipling, Mrs Holloway's obsession was with the life of the mind. She punished him for what he thought. She punished him for being talkative, for asking questions all the time, which she described as 'showing off'. He shared a room with her son who did not relent in torment at night for he made Kipling go through the events of the day, caught him out on inconsistencies and reported them the next morning to his mother as 'lies', and justification for a further beating.

Such is Kipling's description of his infant life. The high point of the year was staying with Aunt Georgie and Edward Burne-Jones at the Grange, North End Road, London. He experienced as much love and affection as he could desire and he enjoyed the smell of paints and turpentine from his uncle's studio and games with his two cousins. Other visitors included William Morris and Robert Browning. His aunt Georgie later asked why he had not told her how badly he was being treated but Kipling was unable to answer beyond asserting that *Children tell little more than animals, for what comes to them they accept as eternally established*.[10]

It has been questioned quite how dreadful this life really was, for Trix stayed there for eight years; when his mother took Kipling away, she returned Trix to the place, which she would hardly have done had life there been so abominable. Trix was deeply resentful, however, even though she had to some extent come under Mrs Holloway's spell. The biographer Birkenhead noted that she commented late in life that her parents 'had seen Harry's crafty eyes, they had heard [Mrs Holloway's] false voice; they must have known that she was of the seaside landlady type, and yet they let her be my only teacher and companion until I was ten years old.' Mrs Holloway's lower class and Kipling's recognition of it may have influenced her bad behaviour, as she knew the two children were talking about her when they used such Hindustani words as *Kuch-Nay* or 'low caste nothing-at-all'.

In defence of the Kipling parents, Mrs Holloway encountered Kipling when he was a boisterous and inquisitive child. He was spoiled by his parents and servants and had no idea of how to behave in England. She was unkind and Kipling was not her favourite, but it may be that no more discipline than was usual in English houses was exercised on Kipling. It is probable that Kipling was picked out for particular beatings while Trix was well treated; he certainly always remembered her loyalty in future. Mrs Holloway had no daughter and made a particular pet of Trix who, it seems, began to take on her captor's narrow religiosity. It may well have been that the son of the house was the real villain and his bullying was ignored rather than sanctioned. Both the Kipling children despised him. Kipling felt 'Captain' Holloway's death in 1874, after he had stayed three years at Southsea, was a second abandonment, leaving the spite of Mrs Holloway and Harry unrestrained.

He was to fictionalise his experiences in his early novel *The Light that Failed* but more passionately in the story 'Baa Baa Black Sheep', written 11 years after he left Southsea, where the Black Sheep of the title is a little boy who is treated as Kipling was and he remarks on the effect of the experience: *when young lips have drunk deep of the bitter waters of Hate, Suspicion, and Despair, all the Love in the world will not wholly take away that knowledge.* He tried to leaven this experience when he wrote in *Something of Myself* 60 years after leaving Southsea that his experiences there *drained me of any capacity for real, personal hate for the rest of my days.*[11] This is more wishful thinking than candour; Kipling was severely damaged by his experiences, he could always view them with renewed bitterness, and he was a champion hater all his life.

He was also aware, however, of the preparation this life had given him for the future, *in that it demanded constant wariness, the habit of observation, and attendance on moods and tempers; the noting of discrepancies between speech and action; a certain reserve of demeanour; and automatic suspicion of sudden favours.*[12] His poor eyesight, uncorrected, led to poor schoolwork at the inferior day school to which he was sent. One bad report he threw away and said he had never received it, for which he said Mrs Holloway beat him and sent him to school through the streets of Southsea with the placard 'Liar' on his back. Kipling said that some sort of nervous breakdown followed and Aunt Georgie was sent for. She had already suspected that Kipling had problems one holiday when she saw him hitting out at a hallucination in the garden.

She had a trusted family friend see him, who reported that he was 'half-blind'. After the aunt's departure he was deemed by Mrs Holloway to have been 'showing off' and was segregated from Trix as a punishment.

Like a goddess from the skies, with no warning, Kipling's mother arrived in March 1877 when he was 11. She told him afterwards that when she first came into his room to wish him goodnight, he flung up an arm to guard off the cuff that he had been conditioned to expect. Alice Kipling took him away immediately, to a farm-house on the edge of Epping Forest, where he enjoyed meeting the locals and playing around the farm animals. His cousin Stanley Baldwin came for a six-week stay.

His mother obtained spectacles for him so he could at last realise his educational potential. This corrected one of his problems though his suffering was deep-rooted as his mother may have realised, for she now provided nine months of rural rest and family visits. The problems to be dealt with by this asylum in the country-side were the abandonment by his parents, with a hyper-trophied feeling that for some reason he deserved this treatment. To this torment was added his active imagination, which worked on the images brought into him by his poor eyesight so he was seeing *shadows and things that were not there*.[13]

It has been suggested that there is a short-sighted personality type, that literally the way a person sees affects their attitude to the world, so the far-sighted person is easily able to capture the 'big picture' while those with short-sightedness are skilled at detailed work. Kipling certainly showed in his work a superlative ability to see the minutiae of life, the nuances of speech, the details of relationships. When dealing with the big issues of race, empire and gender, however, he repeatedly failed to bring the same understanding or sensitivity, as if he were looking at a distant, blurred picture.

Another aspect of Kipling's interior life that became apparent at this time was his habit of wakefulness. Like many very prolific workers, he needed little sleep. It was at this time, at the age of 11, that as he put it, *the night got into my head.*[14] He and his mother were staying in a house in the Brompton Road, London when he rose in the middle of the night and wandered about the house till daybreak, watching the sunrise. He was later to discover that the period just before dawn was to be his most creative. All might have been well with this boyhood adventure but it occurred to Kipling that his pet toad Pluto, who lived in his pocket, might be thirsty so the boy stole into his mother's room to give him a drink from the water jug but lost his grip on the jug which dropped and broke, leading to general wakefulness and recriminations.

This was a period of rapid intellectual growth. Kipling was allowed to roam free around the South Kensington Museum (now the Victoria and Albert Museum) to learn the mysterious beauty of things; he could read as much as he wanted, his favourites were Emerson's poems and Bret Harte's stories and a wide variety of verses that he memorised for the future pleasure of remembering them. He could ask the meaning of things from adults without fear and had the joy of being able to take a pen and write without being accused of 'showing off' by doing so. It was soon to come to an end, however, for he was to be sent to boarding school.

Westward Ho!

Kipling's experience of a sub-standard day school at Southsea had not taught him to look forward to going to school. The one that was chosen, within the means of the Kiplings, was the United Services College which had been recently set up at Westward Ho! near Bideford to cater for the limited educational needs of the children of junior officers serving in India. Its head teacher was Cormell Price, a friend of the Kiplings and of the William Morris set. He was charged with running a school whose main objective was to tutor boys to pass the recently instituted army entrance exam and qualify for imperial service.

Despite his artistic inclinations, Price's school was, even by the standards of the day, a primitive establishment. It comprised *twelve bleak houses by the shore*: a row of lodging houses which had been connected by a long covered corridor with a large hall at one end.[15] As Kipling said, *the food would now raise a mutiny in Dartmoor*.[16] However, Kipling was generous enough to the establishment to acknowledge that the regime did them no physical harm; the sick-house was permanently empty except for accidents. There was, he wrote, none of the homosexuality common to public schools or as he put it, *no cases of even suspected perversion.* [17]

During his first years at Westward Ho! Kipling was allowed to go to the Paris Exhibition of 1878, where his father was in charge of Indian Exhibits. His father urged his son to learn French, an accomplishment not then well regarded in English schools where France was seen as a fount of immorality. In literature, he devoured Swinburne and Poe, then progressed to Browning.

His friend George Beresford described how 'a broad smile appeared with a small boy behind it, carrying it about and pointing it in all directions ... a cheery, capering, podgy little fellow, as precocious as ever he could be.' Kipling's spectacles were considered strange on a boy, as at this time such appendages were associated with old age. They gave him the schoolboy nickname of Gig-lamps or Gigger. His face held other marvels: 'When you looked more closely at this new boy, you were astonished to see what seemed to be a moustache right across the smile, and so it was – an early spring moustache just out of the ground of his upper lip.'[18] Kipling already had the beetling eyebrows which, with his heavy moustache, were to characterise his face in later life.

Kipling suffered from bullying and as a short-sighted boy new to a school environment, his first months were a trial, but he was a fast developer and was quickly strong enough to resist the aggressors. As he and Beresford grew older they felt they merited a study and obtained permission to convert a box room into a space for themselves and one other. The third was Lionel Dunsterville, an adventurous youth, from an army family who was to be a lifelong friend of Kipling. Kipling's spontaneous affection for his friends is refreshing, *They took up room on tables that I wanted for writing; they broke into my reveries; they mocked my Gods; they stole, pawned or sold my outlying or neglected possessions; and – I could* not have gone on a week without them nor they without me.[19]

Kipling first fictionalised his school experiences in magazine stories published in 1897–9, later issued as Stalky & Co, which was dedicated to his old headmaster Cormell Price. Other Stalky stories were added up to 1929. As he left the United Services College in 1882, and the first were written 15 years later, it was hardly a contemporaneous account. In the stories Dunsterville, who went on to be a soldier, is Stalky; Beresford, who would later become a civil engineer, is William M'Turk; and Beetle is a self-portrait. Their exploits mainly concerned a boyish enthusiasm for going out of school bounds for poaching and teenage experiment with drugs – alcohol and tobacco in this case.

The stories have more literary than biographical relevance and belong to a prolific stage in Kipling's writing career to be considered later, but it is relevant that throughout the stories, as doubtless throughout his schooldays, runs a conscious perception that the tricks, japes, adventures and feats of daring in which the boys take part have a real and specific relevance to the outside world. The United Services College was a training ground for those who would maintain the Empire and the boys never forgot it in work or in play, though their consciousness of the need to earn their living meant there was more dedicated hard work than at most public schools. The Stalky of the title, for example, was given his name because of his elaborate practical jokes, which he played out leaving no evidence of the perpetrator, and were therefore the provenance of a scout or stalker in the field of battle. Kipling relates in his autobiography *Something of Myself* that he sees Stalky as 'Commander-in-Chief and Chief of his own Staff', even at 13 seeing himself as a first-person witness of the activities of others, an admirer of powerful men rather than the hero of his own life.

The boys' view of the imperial mission was fiercely realistic, so that Stalky's remarks in 'A Little Prep' on finding the school sergeant Foxy in mourning for a former pupil seem a brutal response: *'By Gum!' quoth Stalky, uncovering as he read. 'It's old Duncan – Fat Sow Duncan – killed on duty at something or other Kotal. "Rallyin' his men with conspicuous gallantry." He would, of course. "The body was recovered." That's all right. They cut 'em up sometimes … Poor old Fat-Sow! I was a fag when he left. How many does that make to us, Foxy?'*

'Mr Duncan, he is the ninth.'

Intellectually, Kipling continued his delight in Tennyson, Browning and Swinburne though not, interestingly enough, the fourth 'great' of the mid-Victorian period, the more contemplative Matthew Arnold. In fiction he devoured Dickens, Thackeray, Defoe and Fielding, but also Smollett and Bunyan. In terms of artistic style he was influenced by developments of the Pre-Raphaelite movement that had engaged his uncle and father. This was transforming itself while he was at school into the aesthetic movement and, in contrast to the severe style of sports-loving schoolboys, the Kipling set decorated their study in olive green and grey-blue, scouring curio shops to find old oak carvings, ancient prints and pieces of old china. Kipling was sufficiently aware of Oscar Wilde to write a poem, 'Ave Imperatrix', with the same title and themes as that used by the young Irishman.

Sexually he matured early, as the evidence of facial hair showed: he was soon a very hairy youth and was, as he let slip once, *not innocent in some respects, as the fish girls of Appledore could have testified had they chosen*, though whether this was kissing, fondling or more adventurous activities is impossible to tell.[20] Kipling packed a good deal into his four years at the United Services College, fully forming characteristics which were to be apparent throughout his life. His poetic industry was prodigious: while still 16 he had a sonnet published in a periodical, *The World*, he was contributing to the *United Services Chronicle*, which he edited, and his mother was collecting enough of his verse in India for a book. At school he developed his love of male comradeship which was to be a part of many works; an unfortunate tendency to hero-worship; and he had started a pattern of unsuccessful love matches with strong women.

In 1880 when 14, Kipling took a trip to Southsea to visit Trix. He met her friend Florence Garrard, a Pre-Raphaelite, slender girl with pale skin, long dark hair, large grey eyes and a boyish figure. Kipling was instantly smitten with a love that would last 11 years and inform his attitude to women for the rest of his life.

Trix described her as 'very slender with a long plait of brown hair, as thick as your arm, and the same thickness all the way down, swinging below her knees. Her head was too small for her body, her hair too heavy for her head, hair like Rapunzel; her eyes too big for her face, such eyes, of the true grey with no hint of blue or hazel, and the thickest, straightest black lashes I have ever seen. An ivory pallor that never flushed or changed but always looked healthy. The mouth in repose was a straight line, and the small features as delicate as a cameo. She gave most of her dress allowance to her sister, who always looked like a rag-bag, and fluttered out of doors like a worrycrow, or bird-scarer, while she [Flo] wore old Holland dresses or the simplest blue serge.'[21] 'It keeps her happy' Flo said of her sister, 'and I hate fuss and feathers; if I had a best hat, Bequot [her pet goat] would eat it and perhaps die.'[22] Trix said 'her elder sister was common enough to bring fur to one's teeth but Flo was a darling.' [23]

A member of the family who owned the jewellers Garrard and Co, Flo was more than a year older than Kipling, but had been brought up in continental hotels so was more sophisticated and with a maddeningly elusive, self-centred manner. She smoked cigarettes, was careless of her appearance and explained that she came from a hopeless family, both her father and mother had delirium tremens, her sister suffered from curvature of the spine and incipient sex mania.[24] Trix later called her 'a curious blend of simplicity and sophistication, wisdom and ignorance. A gift of natural refinement stood in the place of religion and of home training.' Trix did not remember any interest in drawing, she practised the piano conscientiously but had no love of music, hardly read anything and was a poor letter writer, which surprised Trix who was a superior writer though she was four years younger than Flo. Her goat, 'she loved whole-heartedly and the only time she was ever cross with me was when she feared I was winning Bequot's affections away from her.'[25]

Kipling immediately realised that he must overcome her stand-offishness, which he originally attributed to his comparative youth. Soon after meeting Flo he wrote her a poem with a rhyme scheme and subject matter drawn from Swinburne's 'Dolores', including the stanza,

We have met, and the meeting is over;
We must part, and the parting is now;
We have played out the game – I, boy lover,
In earnest, and you, dearest, how?

He had much to offer: she was a student at a local art school, he was intimate with the Poynter and Burne-Jones families and collaborated with the Morris and Burne-Jones children on their family magazine *The Scribbler*. He had little experience of girls, however, and Flo became the light of his life, an idolised image who was to overshadow his emotional life for many years.

His relationship with Flo was to become part of a novel, *The Light that Failed*, so all of his early life found its way into fiction, showing a true writer's ability to make the best of the experiences which life served up to him. He must have thought ruefully of his cousin Stanley Baldwin who went to Harrow, but he did not spend his school days in the sullen sulk of the poor relation.

Baldwin then went on effortlessly to Trinity, Cambridge, to idle away his time towards a third-class degree.

Kipling's family could no more afford a university place for their clever son than they could afford a good school. Kipling toyed with the idea of becoming a doctor and spent some time on what would later be called 'work experience' at St Mary's, Paddington, which was more material for the writer in him, but it did not bring out the physician.

Flo was more of an inspiration, such that he presented her with a collection of his verse, many of them inspired by love, transcribed in a book he facetiously titled *Sundry Phansies Writ by One Kipling*.

Cormell Price spoke to the 16-year-old Kipling in the summer of 1882 to tell him his future: at the end of the summer term he was to go to India to work on a newspaper in Lahore, where his parents now lived, and he would receive 100 silver rupees a month. Kipling arranged to see Flo and begged her to marry him. It is impossible to know exactly what happened at that meeting, but when Kipling left on the *Brindisi* from Tilbury on 20 September 1882 he was under the impression he was engaged to Flo Garrard.

The Family Square

Completing his month-long journey at Bombay in October 1882, Kipling's sense of the sight and smell and sound of India was revitalised, so that he began to say sentences in the vernacular whose meaning he did not know: his past had sprung up again within him, he had come home. He still had four days' rail travel to Lahore during which, he said, his *English years fell away, nor ever, I think, came back in full strength.*[26]

While Kipling was at Southsea, in 1875, his father had accepted the post of head of the Mayo School of Industrial Art at Lahore and curator of the Lahore Museum, which was described as the Wonder House in Kipling's novel *Kim*. The Museum stood in a broad avenue between the whitewashed walls of the European quarter and the cobbled lanes of the ancient Indian walled city of Lahore; opposite it was the Kipling family's bungalow in a compound of its own – therefore neither in the European nor the native quarter. The military cantonment of Mian Mir stood nearby.

Kipling looked older than his years, the appearance accentuated by the whiskers he had grown since leaving school, which his mother ordered to be removed immediately. Henceforward Kipling himself did not have to shave while in India as his servant gently shaved him while he slept.

Kipling suffered the peculiar experience of meeting his mother and father as virtual strangers and he had genuince fears that he simply might not like these people whose lives he had not shared for ten years. Fortunately he found his mother *delightful* and his father *a humorous, tolerant and expert fellow-craftsman*. He had his own room, horse, cart and groom, and his own servant, handed over to him by his father's servant, whose son he was, *with the solemnity of a marriage contract*.[27] They delighted more in the company of each other than with strangers, and when Trix joined them, in 1884, the family was complete. She wrote that she had never laughed so much, before or since, as when she spent evenings at home with her brother and they played elaborate games. On Shakespeare evenings all talk was forbidden except quotations from Shakespeare, though Kipling was an unparalleled improviser so Trix grew to mistrust his parodies of Elizabethan jargon. She taught him to dance, which was not, she surmised, a part of the curriculum at Westward Ho!. She said, 'He was so happy at home. He had his horse, his dog and dog-cart and the three of us loving and admiring him. I never remember him losing his temper all those years.'[28]

The Civil and Military Gazette, recently set up as a daily paper based in Lahore, was financed by Lockwood Kipling's friend George Allen, who had arranged for Rudyard Kipling to be interviewed in London. Kipling's defective eyesight left him unfit for any kind of government service, but as he had a gift for language his father thought he had better become a journalist.

He was, he found when he arrived, one of two

editorial staff of the one daily paper of the Punjab – the other was the editor Stephen Wheeler – and Kipling worked for ten to 15 hours a day. *A daily paper comes out every day even though fifty per cent of the staff have fever,* he wrote. Through his fever and chronic dysentery he discovered that it was possible to work with a temperature of 104 degrees, even though he had to ask the office the next day who had written the article. Many of his contemporaries in the Punjab were to die, *from typhoid mostly at the regulation age of twenty-two.*[29] When there was an outbreak of 11 cases of typhoid in their white community of 70, they felt themselves lucky to lose only four.

Kipling struggled with native compositors who knew no English and drunken proofreaders. He loathed Wheeler, whose task it was to make a reporter out of him, but acknowledged that he owed whatever he knew of accuracy and application to the older man. The editor had found his young charge (who had been foisted on him by his proprietor) excessively literary and endeavoured to beat this out of him with a gruelling routine of turning news agency telegrams into printable copy.

He covered race meetings, the opening of bridges and other big structures, floods on the railways, village festivals, cholera outbreaks and communal riots, viceregal visits, murder and divorce trials and something he described as *a really filthy job: an inquiry into the percentage of lepers among the butchers who sold beef and mutton to the European community of Lahore.*[30] He learned how to work with the sensibilities of different communities and castes, to resist bribes and to take and give a rebuke in an Indian way which gave no offence.

His first taste of bribery came when he was called to the home of an old Afghan warrior who was in exile in Lahore for having fought against the British. As Kipling explained in a letter to his aunt, with grandiloquent compliments the Afghan appealed to the teenage sub-editor to write of the injustice of keeping him in Lahore while his wives were in Kabul: he should be allowed to return.

His story was interesting enough and could have formed the basis of a piece in the *Civil and Military Gazette*, but the Afghan made the mistake of handing Kipling a bundle of 16,000 rupees (about £1,300). After such an insult, Kipling could not write the requested article but he daren't remonstrate with the man in his own house so he handed back the notes saying he was not one of the lower races, but an English sahib.

The Afghan concluded that the bribe was not appropriate, but since all sahibs valued women and horses he called for seven fine horses to be displayed, and asked Kipling to pick three. He also called for a beautiful Kashmiri girl who Kipling took the opportunity of kissing while the Afghan's back was turned. Kipling admitted to being tempted but he eventually cursed the Afghan for attempting to blacken his name and went to leave, only to find under his horse's saddle a bag of uncut sapphires and emeralds, which he pitched through a window. He rode back past the European settlement where people were pouring out of church, remarking to himself that he *may be able to help the old boy respectably and without any considerations.*[31]

In an event rather more telling about the reporter's place in the scheme of things, Kipling was sent to the native state of Patialia to report on the visit there of the Viceroy, Lord Ripon. At the end of the visit Kipling was presented with a gift of fruit and nuts with a bribe of 1,000 rupees at the bottom. He immediately went to tackle the officials responsible and returned the notes to the finance minister, angry that he had been treated like a servant. Two other reporters present accepted their bribe, *but they were half-castes*, as Kipling said.[32] He clearly had to put as much distance as he could between himself and such fellow newspaper professionals.

The other side of the work was his technical administration of composition and printing, which the teenager frequently had to take on because the editor had fever. One monsoon night he was at home at 10 pm but could not rest for wondering what was happening at the print works, so he left the house and splashed over to the press. As he had feared, mutiny was in the offing with the men *saying they wouldn't work any more and C. was tearing his hair over the advertisements. Ram Dass said he was cold and hungry and eyed the brandy bottle.* Kipling encouraged the men to work all night by rolling up his sleeves and getting stuck in himself. The two-colour title page was not printing on the worn-out type, requiring him to improvise a support with gum and paper; then he needed to correct the proofs of everything, even the advertisements. He then went round encouraging the workforce, telling them such work had never been done in India before and that they put the rival Calcutta printers to shame. He got to bed at 5.30 am but was still up, though late, for breakfast with his family.[33]

He joined the Punjab club at the age of 17 and was therefore in the company of those working in the army, railways, forestry, engineering, irrigation, medicine and the law, so he was able to absorb technical information, patterns of speech and stories about people which were to become the fabric of his Indian stories. He was also invited into the Freemasons, by a special dispensation as in 1885 he was under age at 19, but they needed a secretary and thought he would fit the bill. Here he was to meet, on an equal footing, as well as the white Christians of Empire, Muslims, Hindus, Sikhs, a Jew and members of the reform theistic Hindu movement the Brahmo Samaj. It was another world opening up to Kipling, and it is convincingly argued that Masonic symbols and themes occur in many of Kipling's stories.[34] The Masons also satisfied Kipling's need for a sense of religion which was not dogmatic, and provided him with a reliable set of contacts in every country he was to visit in his many travels in the future.

He did not always swim easily in European circles. His coarse upbringing at the United Services College had given him no social graces and had led him into a habit of frequent swearing, which was tedious. His visual disability meant he had never played games to any degree, which excluded him from the company of those who thought about little else. Like many people who are emotionally insecure, he was aggressively superior, resisting contact with others before they had a chance to get close and potentially to reject him. Though moving in an adult world, he was an adolescent, unsure of his place and his powers. He was once thrown downstairs by two men at the club, irritated by an evening of his self-important persiflage.

In the night wanderings that became his habit he discovered the nightlife of India when it was too hot to sleep. He was criticised in the European community for moving among the natives, but he was protected from censure by the fact that however hard he tried to fit in with their society, he would never be one with the smart army officers and the government officials at the gymkhanas and polo matches. There was therefore no particular incentive to try, and he could follow his own path; he was *the cat that walked by himself*, taking the advice he would later give *down to Gehenna or up to the throne, he travels fastest who travels alone*.

He described in a letter to a friend how he had fallen in love with India, *my own place where I find heat and smells and oils and spices, and puffs of temple incense, and sweat and darkness, and dirt and lust and cruelty, and above all, things wonderful and fascinating innumerable.*[35] Kipling discovered an ability to immerse himself in native life, to know the ways and language of the bazaar so well that he could move in that environment naturally without troubling to translate. He later remembered, *I would wander till dawn in all manner of odd places – liquorshops, gambling- and opium-dens, which are not a bit mysterious, wayside entertainments such as puppet shows, native dances; or in and about the narrow gullies under the Mosque of Wazir Khan for the sheer sake of looking. Sometimes, the Police would challenge, but I knew most of their officers, and many folk in some quarters knew me for the son of my Father, which in the East more than* anywhere else is useful … One would come home, just as light broke, in some night-hawk of hired carriage which stank of hookah-fumes, jasmine-flowers, and sandalwood; and if the driver were moved to talk, he told one a good deal. Much of real Indian life goes on in the hot-weather nights. That is why the native staff of the offices are not much use next morning.[36]

In the intense heat he had six punkah wallahs working fans in relays round the clock to keep his bedroom cool. Kipling felt it was well worth petting them and remarked, They have a child's weakness for sweets (serves 'em instead of flesh meat) and 31/2 pence give them all oceans of sticky sweet cakes.[37]

Kipling's time at the United Services College gave him an easy manner with soldiers and in Lahore the military became another of the worlds in which he was able to move effortlessly. He first visited the barracks of the 2nd Battalion Fifth Fusiliers, for example, where an orderly officer friend had taken him to meet the colour sergeant and be introduced to some of the men with a view to writing about army life. Here he was able to follow the patterns of speech and mannerisms of professional soldiers. The fruits of these excursions were the 18 Soldiers Three stories about the trio of soldiers who were supposedly three friends of Kipling, but were in fact a composite of many soldiers he met.

He considered that private soldiers endured unnecessary torments on account of doctrinaire Christians who, on grounds of piety, resisted moves to have the bazaar prostitutes inspected for disease or the men taught how to avoid VD. This official virtue cost our army in India nine thousand expensive white men a year always laid up from venereal disease.[38] He developed a keen sympathy for the bare horror of the private soldier's life and became so known for his compassionate interest that as a young man he was invited by the Commander-in-Chief, Lord Roberts, well known for his sympathy for the common soldier, to give his feelings about the men's opinions of their accommodation.

He came to know the rites and celebrations of the army, often dining with subalterns at meals beginning with 30 grains of quinine in the sherry to ward off malaria. An early biographer, Lord Birkenhead, remarked that it was at this time that Kipling 'conceived his life-long devotion to the army, and his intense veneration of the man of action to the detriment of the thinker and intellectual.'[39] Kipling certainly idolised the soldiers in whose mess he often ate; and there is a certain amount of self-loathing in his devotion to a calling from which he is excluded by his physical defect of poor eyesight. Much of the brutality of his work seems to relate back to Kipling's willingness to suppress his finer feelings in order to sit at the tables of the beefy giants able and willing to die for the Empire.

Beginning to sing

Soon after Kipling returned to India he found his mother had collected and had printed a collection of his verse under the title Schoolboy Lyrics. Kipling flew into a rage and sulked for two days and none of the verses were reprinted in standard editions of his verse, which gives an indication of how he felt about his juvenilia.

He was busy assimilating experience and establishing himself in his profession as a journalist, but always with an eye to creative writing. He described for his Aunt Edith, the youngest of the Macdonald sisters and the only one unmarried, the life of the reporter who never ceased from writing, for the 'par-boiled' young man would recover the soul of a poet at the end of the day when the telephone stopped ringing.

He composed stories and poems for the *Gazette*, which were rarely subject to profound critical attention in the office. Rukn-Din, the foreman of the print works, was a *Muslim of culture* and responded positively to Kipling's work: *'Your potery is very good sir; just coming proper length today. You giving more soon? One-third column just proper. Always can take on third page.'*[40] The ease with which he found a niche for his light verse was, of course, a result of the frequency with which such verse from a variety of sources appeared in newspapers; Kipling was just the best of the versifiers, always able to beat out some stanzas. What set him apart was not merely his ability to produce topical rhymes (many verse and song writers are so technically accomplished) but his refusal to be satisfied with this alone and determination to improve his work and produce real poetry. Some of his light verse was later published as *Echoes*, a collection of 39 parodies by Kipling and Trix, most of them written by him but all composed under the incisive criticism of Alice Kipling.

His early work owed much to his family for maintaining an environment in which creativity could flourish. Some of his work was owed to them in a more literal sense. He acknowledged that one of his most quoted lines, *What do they know of England who only England know?* was taken from his mother and Trix remarked that *East is East and West is West and never the twain shall meet* should also be attributed to Alice Kipling. His use of his family's words was quite open according to Trix; he would call out *O! good, bags I* when he was taken with a particular phrase which he wished to use. Kipling was a 'persistent pen-biter' according to his sister, in every room in their house was a writing table and every table had a tray of pens, each one 'bitten into a faggot at the end.'[41]

The newspaper's management allowed Kipling to write for publications whose circulation did not compete with that of the *Civil and Military Gazette* and thereby both earned some extra cash and spread his name further around the sub-continent. He wrote ephemeral verse for a variety of Indian newspapers, often under pseudonyms, more than 20 of which have been identified. One paper, the Allahabad *Pioneer*, offered to take anything he cared to send them.

In his second year of adult work, the 18-year-old Kipling sent his regards to his cousin Stanley Baldwin and remarked wistfully, *I'd give something to be in the Sixth at Harrow as he is, with a University Education to follow.*[42] His exclusion from academic education continued to rankle; it was tactless of an incompetent Indian clerk who handled the *Gazette*'s accounts to remind Kipling that he had been to university. The perennially sensitive Kipling took him to task and later fumed in a letter, *Knows fractions and decimals – can't keep the register of* two hundred orders correctly or neatly – Remembers The Deserted Village and mislays an account book.[43] These educated Indians, often Bengalis, were known as Babus and their supposed failings an object of ridicule among the Europeans, which attitude helped propel them towards the Indian Nationalist movement. Kipling had no time for the emerging political class who could impress English liberals with their knowledge of English language and culture, but were unwilling to tackle issues in their own society such as child marriage and bad drains. Kipling's superiority was precarious, however; he was not on the lowest rung of Anglo-Indian life, but he was not far up the ladder. He would have to be more than a reporter for a local newspaper writing topical verse to gain the fame he craved.

One night in September 1884 when cholera was rife in Lahore, Kipling was alone in the house and he woke with agonising pains in his stomach and aching limbs. He found himself Threshing round in a pitch dark empty house and calling for servants who won't hear and hunting for medicines one can't find. Eventually he found his man-servant, who lit a lamp, took one look at him and bolted out of the house. Kipling thought this must be the end, his servant had run away for fear of the cholera, and he poured himself a dose of chlorodyne and sat to await the progress of the sickness and to pray for morning. Very soon his servant reappeared carrying a lamp, a bottle and an opium pipe and set to work rolling opium pills to put in the pipe. He insisted Kipling smoke as much as he could, and he soon felt the cramps in his legs dying and his stomach more settled, followed by the blissful oblivion of opium. The next day, though clearly intoxicated with opium, he was fit to get up and go to work. *My man is awfully pleased with himself and walks round me as though I was a rare and curious animal, occasionally putting his hand on my shoulder,* Kipling wrote, *he certainly cut short a spell of the acutest pain I have ever experienced in my life and no woman could have tended me more carefully than he through those terrible hours between eleven and two.*[44]

The experience gave him the personal knowledge necessary to write his first published story, 'The Gate of the Hundred Sorrows', printed in the *Civil and Military Gazette* in September 1884. It is the rambling, stream-of-consciousness monologue of an Anglo-Indian opium addict. Deeply evocative of degradation and listlessness, its depiction of the other characters in the opium den and understanding of the narrator's mind show how Kipling's appreciation of character was deepening.

Stimulated by his limited literary success, Kipling now attempted a more ambitious project, a novel intended to lay bare the seedy underworld of Anglo-Indian life. By 30 July 1885 he had 237 foolscap pages written of *Mother Maturin*, the story of an old Irish woman who kept an opium den in Lahore. At one time he was thinking of having it published in weekly parts in an Indian newspaper, but it was an immense, bulky work, which seemed to have all the faults of a first novel, including a tendency to remain unfinished despite the proud author having advertised it widely among his friends. Parts of it, describing the hot, dark alleys and multifarious activities of the Indian underworld were used in *Kim* but Kipling's skill in prose work was never to be as a novelist; his short stories were his great achievement.

His next two stories were published in *Quartette*, a Christmas 1885 supplement to the *Gazette* by 'Four Anglo- Indian Writers'. The title was a reference to what his mother called The Family Square, wittily uniting a pun on 'family circle' with the fact that there were four of them and the notion of a British Square – the supposedly impregnable battle formation of the army. *Quartette* contained the first two stories by Kipling that he later thought, after revision, worth republishing: 'The Phantom Rickshaw' and 'The Strange Ride of Morrowbie Jukes', both in a style that could be called Indian Gothic, a disturbing world much influenced by Edgar Allen Poe where reality and the paranormal meet.

The tales are full of feverish nights on the hot plains, in characterisation the straightforward and honest Englishmen confronted by the mystery and deviousness of the East. Kipling uses such expressions as *there was a crack in Pansay's head and a little bit of the Dark World came through and pressed him to death* and *Morality is blunted by consorting with the Dead who are alive*.

'The Phantom Rickshaw' was a ghost story, and not a particularly sophisticated one, about a man haunted by a woman he had used and who had died of a broken heart; the other story was a far deeper tale of an Englishman in a fever who rode at night and fell into a pit with sloping sides. In the pit are those hastily taken to the cremation sites at a time of cholera but who then recovered, and were therefore unclean. Jukes is met by an insolent

Indian he had known and beaten previously, who now declares that they will live together in a 'republic', for all are equal in the place of the undead.

At the same time that Kipling was making his first excursions into prose, the family's social standing began to improve. The Earl of Dufferin's appointment as Viceroy in 1884 meant power was in the hands of a more refined and cultured individual than previously and the Kiplings consequently flourished. The Viceroy's daughter, Lady Helen, attended Lockwood's sketching class; the Viceroy enjoyed conversation with Lockwood and was enchanted by Alice Kipling. He paid her the charming compliment of saying 'dullness and Mrs Kipling cannot exist in the same room.'[45] Trix nearly carried off the supreme prize when she became close to the Viceroy's son Lord Clandeboye, but his family spotted the danger signs of romance and sent him away. The good relations between the families remained, however, and those who had passed over Kipling and his family with a superior air fumed to see the social progress they had made. By 1885 the Kiplings were welcome at Simla, the hill station whence the viceregal court moved in the hottest months, making the perch in the mountains into a seat of government.

Another change hastened Kipling's development as a writer: his editor Stephen Wheeler returned to England in 1886, sick of the heat and fevers, and he was replaced by a young man called Kay Robinson, brought in to liven up the dull paper. Robinson had corresponded with Kipling over the newspaper verses they both wrote but his first impression of the writer was disappointing:

'early in 1886 his face had not acquired the character of manhood, and contrasted somewhat unpleasantly with his stoop … his heavy eyebrows, his spectacles, and his sallow Anglo-Indian complexion; while his jerky speech and abrupt movements added to the unfavourable impression. But his conversation was brilliant …' Robinson quickly became not only a colleague but a friend, an important consideration when Kipling was often lonely. In an affectionate portrait of Kipling's working methods he described the young man often taking off his spectacles to wipe them with a handkerchief because he was laughing so much as to cry and mist them up. 'In the heat of summer white cotton trousers and thin vest constituted his office attire, and by the day's end he was spotted all over like a Dalmation dog. He had a habit of dipping his pen frequently and deep into the ink-pot, and as all his movements were abrupt, almost jerky, the ink used to fly. When he darted into my room, as he used to do about one thing or another in connection with the contents of the paper a dozen times in the morning, I had to shout to him to "stand off"; otherwise, as I knew by experience, the abrupt halt he would make, and the flourish with which he placed the proof in his hand before me, would send the penful of ink … flying over me.'[46]

Kipling's first mature book of verse, *Departmental Ditties*, contained pieces on Anglo-Indian life, some of which had appeared in newspapers under the title 'Bungalow Ballads'. The first edition was published in 1886 with the cover looking like a brown official envelope, tied up with 'red tape' and addressed to Heads of

Department and Anglo-Indians from *Rudyard Kipling, Assistant, Department of Public Journalism, Lahore District*. He boasted that *among a pile of papers [it] would have deceived a clerk of twenty years' service*. On the business side he said: *The money came in poor but honest rupees, and was transferred from the publisher, my left-hand pocket, direct to the author, my right-hand pocket. Every copy sold in a few weeks, and the ratio of expenses to profits, as I remember it, has since prevented my injuring my health by sympathising with publishers who talk of their risks and advertisements.*[47]

Kay Robinson took eight volumes to England on leave and sent them to various newspapers. It may have been one of these that received a review in *Longman's Magazine* where the 'melancholy ditties' were praised though the reviewer took no pleasure in the fact that Her Majesty's raj was depicted as being administered by men who were preoccupied with jobs, posts, pensions and the attractions of their neighbour's wives. Kipling can hardly be counted as among the ranks of the revolutionaries, but it is noteworthy that his satires were sharp and genuinely subversive in an autocracy where no official opposition to British administration existed. Kipling's verse told such cases as the man sent off to do two men's work in the heat so his superior could have easy access to his wife; or the ignorant colonel appointed to run the railways over the vastly superior but lower-class candidate.

As a result of the publication of *Departmental Ditties*, Kipling, still only 20, became a celebrity, an experience he at first found exciting. *Strangers in trains, and hotels* and all manner of out of the way places come up to me and say nice things.[48] Not only was Robinson much more to Kipling's liking than his predecessor, but part of the enlivening process was commissioning daily 2,000 word pieces for the middle of the paper, many of which were written by Kipling. The first of these were published under the title Plain Tales from the Hills on 2 November 1886 and Kipling was to write and have published 21 stories in the series between then and 10 June 1887, a rate of one a week.

They comprised Indian stories of natives and native life; army stories; and Simla stories featuring Mrs Hauksbee, the shrewd, knowing older woman beloved of Kipling. She was clever, witty, brilliant and sparkling beyond most of her kind; but possessed of many devils of malice and mischievousness, which could be a description of Alice Kipling.[49] While it is refreshing to see an older woman enshrined in fiction, Mrs Hauksbee's celebrated guile is used to secure advancement for second-rate men who flatter her, or obtain the attentions of a young man at a ball.

An even more cloying portrait of an older woman was given in the story of 'Venus Annodomini', who exists only to enjoy the adoration of younger men. The very slight story is that one admirer young enough to be her son is nonplussed to find when his father visits that he had adored the same woman 20 years previously.

All Kipling's close female relationships, with the obvious exception of that with Trix, were with older women. He delighted in the unobtainable, writing that he sought a lady well versed in domestic knowledge, not less than twelve years my senior, and by preference, some other man's wife.[50] What moved him to this adoration of older women is a matter of conjecture but it is reasonable to suggest that it related back to his longing for a mother figure while a child in the House of Desolation.

One of the principal models for the witty and alluring Mrs Hauksbee was Isabella Burton, wife of an intelligence officer, a lively intelligent woman who was able to talk philosophy and literature with Kipling. She also encouraged him to see in the Indian scene not just events and personal interactions, but the motives behind them: for social advancement, promotion or sexual opportunity.

Kipling wrote to Mrs Burton asking if he could dedicate the collection Plain Tales from the Hills to her; the intended dedication To the wittiest woman in India I dedicate this book would obviously lead to her and it was courteous to ask. He is also, however, said by Trix to have told their mother she was the dedicatee: it is most likely that both are true and he paid the compliment to both women in the hope they would not meet and confer.

He had no difficulty in finding a publisher for Plain Tales – he actually had a choice of publisher. The book contained 40 stories, the 29 which had been published under the Plain Tales title in the Civil and Military Gazette; three which had appeared in the newspaper before the Plain Tales series started; and eight new stories. It is one of those books that is more than the sum of its parts: some of the individual stories are not strong, but together they add up to a comprehensive picture of Anglo-India. The publication of Plain Tales as a book was to cement Kipling's reputation in India and its later publication in London was to create one there. Oscar Wilde, reviewing it in *The Nineteenth Century* in the third quarter of 1890 wrote, 'As one turns over the pages of Plain Tales from the Hills one feels as if one were seated under a palm-tree reading life by superb flashes of vulgarity. The jaded, second-rate Anglo-Indians are in exquisite incongruity with their surroundings. The mere lack of style in the storyteller gives an odd journalistic realism to what he tells us. From the point of view of literature Mr Kipling is a genius who drops his aspirates. From the point of view of life he is a reporter who knows vulgarity better than anyone has ever known it ... He is our first authority on the second-rate.'

Physically, by the age of 20 Kipling was a slight man of five and a half feet and just under eight and a half stone. His relentless energy and jerky mannerisms made his appearance a contrast to the urbane narrator of *Plain Tales from the Hills*, who often appears as a character to comfort a jilted woman or enjoy the confidences of a colonel.

As various descriptions of him as 'caddish' demonstrate, he was still a callow youth with much to learn of social grace, humility and tact. He was never backward in asserting his views, often in the company of others who knew the world rather better than he did. He took a lively interest in European girls, dancing with them and sometimes even sending them verses, but kept the image of Flo Garrard before him. *I flirted with the bottled up energy of a year on my lips*, he wrote to aunt Edith about a visit to the social scene at Simla. *Don't be horrified for there were about half a dozen of 'em and I took back the* lacerated fragments of my heart … and returned the whole intact, to Flo Garrard's keeping as per usual.[51]

It was a miserably one-sided relationship, the correspondence of which he later described in the form of a lament about a probably imaginary girl he called 'My Lady' but who is recognisably Flo: I don't wait for her letters, he wrote, I get one, and go on till I get the next, my nose to the grindstone for fear of thinking. When a horrible Sunday comes and I am thrown back upon myself, I know how long I have waited and then I get all the arrears of suspense in one gloomy lump. I have written and told her that, save and except her letters, I have nothing, – absolutely nothing, and that is a fact. The fictional 'Lady' was not generous with her correspondence: My Lady does not favour me with any lengthy outpourings. She doesn't gush and I try in my letters to her to keep myself within that decent insular reserve that is the hereditary mask of the Englishman.[52] The very indifference of a woman is therefore taken as a spur to greater devotion rather than a signal that he should look elsewhere.

In a story, 'On the Strength of a Likeness' he pondered the uses of unrequited love for a young man: It makes him feel important and business-like, and blasé and cynical; and whenever he has a touch of liver, or suffers from want of exercise, he can mourn over his lost love, and be very happy in a tender, twilight fashion. One of Kipling's adored older women was Mrs Maunsell, wife of a colonel, to whom the writer was attracted only because she bore a resemblance to Flo, a shallow relationship he drew on for this story. As a true professional he was always spinning his experiences into gold.

In July 1884 Flo wrote to put an end to what he considered their engagement, or to terminate a tiresome correspondence. Quite why she chose this time is not obvious, it could have been linked with the death of her grandfather, giving her a generous inheritance, but Flo was not the sort to base her actions on money; she had never cared much for material things. It was unlikely that Kipling was rejected because he was a poor prospect financially; it is more probable that the maturing Flo was examining her own personality and deciding that Kipling was not for her.

Kipling and Flo were almost comically mismatched. Trix reported that Flo hardly read a thing; Kipling's sister was disappointed to find that her friend was unable to write a letter at anything above a childish level. Kipling might be one of the finest writers of his generation but it was to no avail if the object of his desires had no respect for the written word. It may have been, also, that Flo was never going to marry any man, perhaps because she was wedded to her art, or perhaps because that was not her inclination.

Now, approaching 20, he had to face the future without the wife back home. He explored his options in fiction, in particular in a bitter story, 'In the Pride of His Youth', where a man leaves his young wife and baby to go to work in India where he struggles to make do, sending much of his meagre salary back home, until the baby dies and the wife goes off with another man. By this time the husband's diligence is rewarded and he is offered a promotion with sufficient remuneration to bring wife and child to India, if he still had them. Now, however, he feels he has *missed the pleasure of youth* and *would go to the Devil*.

Kipling was unable to make a clean break from Flo. Later that year he was pathetically writing to his cousin Margaret Burne-Jones to ask her to enquire about Flo at the Slade School of Art. *I want to know how she is and what she is doing. So far as I know youre [sic] the only person who's likely to be able to find this out for me, and if possible I want you as quietly and unobtrusively as possible to learn all you can about the girl.*[53] The wound inflicted by his love for Flo would not heal, and he would return to it, both in fiction and in ill-advised attempts to see her. Two years later he was still counting time from the point when Flo gave him his 'jawab' (dismissal) and *the bottom had tumbled out of the Great Universe.*[54]

India offered sexual outlets, as Kipling knew well from his meanderings in the City of Night, as he called the walled city of Lahore, after James Thomson's poem. One cryptic account of such an event was described in a diary he kept in 1885. He was in Simla in August, a sojourn that was part holiday though he was also writing sketches of expatriate life in the hills. At one time he had a room next to a couple called Hayes whose noisy sex life troubled him. *Wish they wouldn't put married couple next door to me with one half plank between*, he wrote, *Saps one's morality* and the following day added, *Same complaint. This is really ghastly*. For the next few days, August 4–5, the diary suggests a visit to a prostitute and fears for the consequences: *My own affair entirely. A wet day but deuced satisfactory … Begin to think I've been a fool but aint certain*. Back in Lahore he sought the opinion of

Templeton Young, a doctor of his acquaintance. *He is sanguine and hopeful. I also. More anticipation.* He wrote on 26 August, when he was doubtless told that if he had no symptoms after three weeks the likelihood of his having either major venereal disease was much reduced. The following day he wrote, *First period probation over. Mind easier. Now to look about me.* This last reference relates to 'looking about' for a wife.[55]

Special Correspondent

In autumn 1887 Kipling was ordered to Allahabad to work on a larger paper, the *Pioneer*, owned by the same newspaper group. His salary would be increased and he was to be a 'special correspondent' with a licence to roam as he felt fit.

He had moved from the Muslim and Sikh Punjab to the largely Hindu United Provinces, which was also the home of the Nehru family and a centre of nationalist activity: the Indian National Congress met there in 1888 with 1,400 delegates calling for greater power for the Indian middle class. Kipling was chronicling the ways of an empire at its height, but also of an empire whose days were numbered.

The move was truly his literary break because he was asked to edit the digest of the paper, *The Week's News*, which had a fiction page that included bought-in stories. Kipling saw no need to buy in material when he could manufacture it himself. His literary effort, already impressive, became prodigious, with sometimes three pieces of journalism, poetry or literary prose being written in a week; occasionally it would be one per day.

The most important personal influence on his life now became Edmonia Hill, the wife of Aleck Hill, Professor of Science at Muir Central College and an amateur photographer. Edmonia, known as Ted, was eight years older than Kipling, a lively, attractive woman from Beaver, Pennsylvania. He met her after he had gone to Benares and Calcutta looking for material for travel sketches on the native states (those not ruled directly by Britain) using the rather arch pen name of The Englishman and referring to himself in the third person. When the pieces appeared there was much dinner table conversation as to the identity of the writer, and at one such dinner party Kipling was introduced to Ted as the author. 'Of course I was at once interested' she later recollected, describing him as 'a short, dark-haired and moustached man of uncertain age, wearing very thick glasses.'[56] He flattered her and asked her about America; she invited him to join in badminton and tennis matches and he politely declined. Over the next months they became close confidantes and, when she went to Simla for the heat, almost daily correspondents. The letters give an impression of his usual method of flirtation, showing intense interest in the things which interested Ted, flattering American writers and inviting her to comment on his ideas for stories, thereby bringing her into the conspiracy of writer against the world.

One illuminating subject of correspondence was Kipling's recounting of his conversations with Captain Beames of the 19th Bengal Lancers, who used to visit the writer to talk at length about the vicissitudes of his love affair with a 17-year-old girl. Kipling pillaged the confidences mercilessly for material for his story of the Gadsbys and, while doing it, discussed them in letters to Ted. He also wrote of an adored My Lady who had captured his heart, but the love had not come to fruition – it has been suggested that this too was a fiction, and My Lady was Ted herself, married and unobtainable. Writing about My Lady (the same appellation he used for Flo Garrard) meant he could keep Ted's interest in him by a natural process of jealousy.

These experiences and emotions of 1887 to 1888 provided Kipling with a seemingly inexhaustible flow of material, such that the publisher of his newspaper, A H Wheeler & Co, quickly realised there was an advantage in getting them out in bulk in an easily purchasable form. There was such an appetite for the material that by the end of 1888 they had published six booklets authored by Kipling in paper wrappers under the title *The Indian Railway Library*. They each contained from four to nine short stories, to a total of 38, many of which had first appeared in *The Week's News*. They cost one rupee each, and the appearance of such a mass of Kipling's work at an affordable price, deliberately engineered for railway consumption, meant the reading market was flooded with Kipling's work that year.

The first of them was *Soldiers Three*, seven stories published in paper covers. They were supplemented over the years to a total of 18 by other stories about the same characters. The first offering was dedicated by Kipling to *that very strong man, T Atkins, Private of the Line*. They announced they were *setting forth certain passages in the lives and adventures of privates Terence Mulvaney, Stanley Ortheris and John Learoyd*, Irishman, Yorkshireman and Cockney.

The critic Andrew Lang said Kipling had discovered new kinds of characters including 'his invention of the

British soldier in India.' Kipling may love Thomas Atkins 'but his affection has not blinded him to the faults of the beloved. Mr Atkins drinks too much, is too careless a gallant in love, has been educated either too much or too little, and has other faults ...but he is still brave, when he is well led; still loyal, above all, to his "trusty chum" ... Nobody ever dreamed of telling us all this, till Mr Kipling came.'[57]

Kipling's influence on the soldiers themselves was perhaps even more striking. Sir George Younghusband, who served in India for many years, recalled that when Kipling's work first appeared he knew no soldiers who expressed themselves like his characters. 'Many a time did I ask my brother Officers whether they had ever heard them. No, never. But sure enough, a few years after the soldiers thought, and talked, and expressed themselves exactly like Rudyard Kipling had taught them in his stories!' Kipling's imitators continued with the work 'and they have between them manufactured the cheery, devil-may-care, lovable person enshrined in our hearts as Thomas Atkins. Before he had learned from reading stories about himself that he, as an individual, possessed the above attributes, he was mostly ignorant of the fact. My early recollections of the British soldier are of a bluff, rather surly person, never the least jocose or light-hearted, except perhaps when he had too much beer ... Kipling made the modern soldier.'[58]

More senior ranks also experience Kipling's influence. In one of the other *Railway Library* booklets the story 'Only a Subaltern' describes Bobby Wick, a junior officer who was *taught there was no crime blacker than* that of bringing shame on the Regiment which was the best-shooting, best-drilled, best-set-up, bravest, most illustrious, and in all respects most desirable Regiment within the compass of the Seven Seas. Wicks is a fine man who is prepared to serve his regiment in any way necessary but Kipling does not have him holding the line in the heat of battle or overcoming enemies in hand-to-hand combat. He has his hero dying of cholera before he has even fired a shot. Yet he is still manifestly heroic, and by his presence in dangerous climes is doing the unglamorous work of Empire.

The presentation of an idealised youth may be mawkish to post-1918 generations but it was the presentation of such skill and affection of a decent, loyal, honest Englishman that, as Charles Carrington wrote, 'he moulded a whole generation of young Englishmen into that type. They rose up in their thousands in 1914, and sacrificed themselves in the image that Kipling had created.'[59]

Even in very early Kipling, there are clear indications that his vision of Empire was more sophisticated than that presented by Henty and Haggard. The Man Who Would Be King, a long story which was first published in one of the Indian Railway Library booklets, starts with Kipling as narrator in a realistic scene where he meets Carnehan, a fellow Mason, on a train, and assists him even though the man perpetrates confidence tricks while in the guise of a newspaper special correspondent, the position Kipling really did hold.

Later Carnehan comes to the narrator's office with his friend Dravot, both former soldiers who want the narrator to witness a vow between them. They promise to abstain from drink and women while they make their bid for fame. After three years Carnehan returns to the newspaper to tell his tale. They have pretended to be traders and have reached Kafiristan, where they used rifles they have carried secretly to secure the ascendancy of one warring tribe against the others. They achieve a kingdom, which Dravot calls an empire, by superior technology but also by superior wit, winning the territory through trickery and brazen self-confidence. Eventually Dravot makes the fatal error of breaking the pledge of abstaining from women, when he wants to take one of the local girls as a wife, she bites him, exposing him as human, and the people rebel.

It has a good claim to being the best story Kipling wrote in India; J M Barrie thought it Kipling's masterpiece. It is set in a tragic mould, as the reader knows when Carnehan begins his story that he is dying and Dravot is already dead. It is a parable of hubris, of empire over-reaching itself with reflections of the empire of Alexander the Great and of the British.

Like other of his stories at this time, including 'Wressley of the Foreign Office' and 'The Story of the Gadsbys' (and looking forward to *The Light that Failed*) the disaster of a man's great work in life hangs on his need for a woman.

In June and July 1888 Kipling was again in Simla, absorbing yet more material. On his return to Allahabad he took up residence in the Hill home, a bungalow called Belvedere set in a large garden. For some weeks in 1888 he was on his own in the house while the Hills were travelling, but solitude did him no good, making him surly and mopish.

It was perhaps this summer, but certainly at this stage of his life, that he had a revelatory experience which he described later as the result of having *come to the edge of all endurance. As I entered my empty house in the dusk there was no more in me except the horror of a great darkness, that I must have been fighting for some days.* [60]

He addressed this mental crisis in a peculiarly literary way. Late that night after struggling with his demons, he picked up a copy of a book by the popular author Walter Besant, *All in the Garden Fair*, about a struggling writer, which he read and re-read to give him literary strength. Kipling compared himself with the hero and realised he need not stay in India. He was as well equipped as the fictional character; *I could go away and measure myself against the doorsills of London as soon as I had money. Therefore I would begin to save money, for I perceived there was absolutely no reason outside myself why I should not do exactly what to me seemed good.* [61]

There were other reasons for him to leave. Kipling had promoted a libel suit with his remarks about a sympathiser with the Indian National Congress; and also managed to irritate both the departing Viceroy with a satirical verse on his retirement and the Commander-in-Chief with printed remarks about his appointments procedure. None of this meant Kipling had to go, but it was an indication of his restlessness and the fact that India – or Anglo-Indian society – was getting a little too small for him. By late June 1888 he was writing, *I am more than* ever set in my determination to go home and quit the Pi [Pioneer] ... The leading paper in India is an excellent thing but there are many things better in this world and I must strike out and find 'em.[62]

There were other reasons for his departure: the heat was a torment and he was advised by his doctor not to spend another summer on the plains. This was not compatible with the job of a reporter, which is to be where he is needed rather than where he is comfortable. He had ample money with his savings from the pieces he had written over the years for other newspapers, and his advance of £200 from the publishers of The Indian Railway Library. Trix had finally become engaged to John Fleming, a soldier working in the Survey Department, so her ties to the family square would invariably be weakened and Kipling's need not be retained.

Before he left, or as part of the leaving process, there was a demon Kipling had to exorcise. The memory of Southsea continued to haunt him and in leaving the family home he had not only to confront the events that had marred his childhood, but indict his parents with them.

The story 'Baa Baa Black Sheep', published in the sixth of the Indian Railway Library series, was the only one of his pieces that was not shown to his family before publication. It describes his terrible experiences at the hands of Mrs Holloway and her son, a literary exercise that provoked genuine suffering in Kipling.

Ted, in whose house he was still staying while he wrote it, wrote to her family, 'It was pitiful to see Kipling living over the experience, pouring out his soul in the story, as the drab life was worse than he could possibly describe it. His eyesight was permanently impaired, and, as he had heretofore only known love and tenderness, his faith in people was sorely tried. When he was writing this he was a very sorry guest, as he was in a towering rage at the recollection of those days.'[63]

On publication, his parents recognised the factual basis of the story immediately and appealed to Trix to say the tale was an exaggeration, but she confirmed its basic veracity. They were upset at what was obviously an accusation of an abnegation of the parental duties of love and care for their children. It broke the family square: Kipling was never again to have such a close working relationship with his family; henceforth he would be his own man.

Passage to England

Kipling was planning to go directly to England but it occurred to him he might see something of the world first and asked to be allowed to accompany the Hills, who were planning to visit the US. The party therefore left Calcutta on 9 March 1889, for San Francisco via Rangoon, Hong Kong and Nagasaki; Kipling was still only 23.

With Kipling's eye to the business side of his work, he made use of his trip by offering the *Pioneer* a series of sketches of his journey. He had a clerk in the Allahabad office cut out the pieces as they appeared in the newspaper and keep them together so he had little difficulty in editing them together to form a travel book, *From Sea to Sea*, published in two volumes. It gave ample room for

Kipling's displays of racial superiority over the Chinese and Japanese: the latter nation he mocked for their work towards modernisation and their supposed lack of firmness of character. His failure to understand this part of the changing world (like his failure to understand the rise of the independence movement in India) is perfectly forgivable in a young man, though as time would tell it was not merely an example of the impatience of youth, but evidence of a life-long shallowness that mars Kipling's non-fiction writing. The work was edited and published ten years after it was written, giving time for reflection and amendment had Kipling felt moved to make use of it.

Another work was already developing within the ever-industrious Kipling. Ted Hill described the inception of *Barrack-Room Ballads* while she was standing by the rail with Kipling on the steamer *Africa*, sailing towards Singapore, 'when he suddenly began to hum "Rum-ti-tum-tra-la" – shaking the ashes from his pipe overboard. I was used to this, knowing something was stirring in his brain. Humming in a musical tone he exclaimed, *I have it, I'll write some Tommy Atkins Ballads* and this idea kept simmering for months, with an occasional outbreak in soldierlike language.'[64]

Landing in San Francisco, the Hills travelled quickly to the relatives in Beaver, Pennsylvania. He made his way slowly across the US, before rejoining the Hills, writing patronising pieces about the Americans for his Anglo-Indian audience. *In a vast marble-paved hall under the glare of an electric light sat forty or fifty men; and for their use and amusement were provided spittoons of infinite* capacity and generous gape. Most of the men wore frock-coats and top-hats – the things that we in India put on at a wedding breakfast if we possessed them, – but they all spat. They spat on principle. The spitoons were on the staircases, in each bedroom – yea, and in chambers even more sacred than these. They chased one into retirement, but they blossomed in chiefest splendour round the Bar, and they were all used, every reeking one of 'em.[65]

His father's extensive array of contacts, garnered from his connections in the art world and the many eminent visitors who had come to see the Lahore Museum, meant Kipling had people to see across the continent. His journey was not, however, a professional success. He had discovered, to his absolute fury, the limits of his control over his own hard work: in a shop in Japan he found an American pirated edition of his own tales. His meeting with Harper, the New York publishing company, showed he still had mountains to climb before achieving acceptance. They dismissed him with a brief letter and the words, 'Young man, this house is devoted to the production of literature.'[66] Kipling would have to produce something very different from the Indian Railway Library to win over the highbrows.

He did, however, make a point of visiting Mark Twain in Elmira, New York, an author almost twice his age whom he had learned to love and admire 14,000 miles away who he later considered the master of us all.[67] Twain learned to admire Kipling and the two were to meet again often, the last time when they were both given honorary doctorates by Oxford in 1907.

Kipling embarked on a ten-day crossing to Liverpool

on 5 October 1889. He could look back on an impressive achievement for a young man. He had published one book of verse, *Departmental Ditties*, one of prose, *Plain Tales from the Hills*, and the six short *Indian Railway Library* books, even though he had not written the all-important novel (he had abandoned *Mother Maturin*) and there was no stability in his emotional life. Had he died now, he would still be remembered as the chronicler of the British in India, a scene he painted as richly as Zola described Second Empire France or Dickens Victorian England. For a man of only 23 the achievement was remarkable.

A Lion in London

As the centre of the largest empire the world had ever known, London was a glittering spectacle of fabulous wealth and learning; of ignorance and squalor. Great public buildings stood streets away from the direst hovels; the theatres and music halls of the West contrasted with the brothels and opium dens of the East End.

Kipling rented two small rooms in the very centre of London, in Villiers Street, off the Strand, a few paces from Trafalgar Square in one direction and the Thames in the other; and a short walk from Piccadilly Circus and Leicester Square.

Despite the grand-sounding name of Embankment Chambers, Kipling's perch was an apartment above a sausage and mash shop, shaken by the trains rumbling into Charing Cross station. He was still surviving on the money he had brought from India but he found he could live frugally. His downstairs neighbour the Sausage King *for tuppence gave as much sausage and mash as would carry one from breakfast to dinner ... another tuppence found me a filling supper*, tobacco was another tuppence, *and fourpence, which included a pewter of beer or porter, was the price of admission to Gatti's*, which was a music hall opposite the sausage shop.[68] Kipling listened, fascinated, to the cab-men and the music hall girls shouting outside in the street and he sat for hours in Gatti's listening to the talk of soldiers, which he wove into the verses of *Barrack-Room Ballads*.

He obtained a huge roll-top desk at which he worked, and he also had a Gurkha knife on which he carved on the desk, from Longfellow 'Oft was I weary, when I toiled at thee'. He would fiddle with the knife when he was working out the details of a story, chopping into the furniture. Ted Hill and Caroline Taylor had helped him to move in, decorating the rooms with oriental rugs and curios he had picked up on his recent travels. Kipling had met and started to flirt with Caroline Taylor, Ted's younger sister, in Beaver, Pennsylvania, at her father's home when he rejoined the Hills to continue the trip to Britain.

Caroline was to go to India with her sister, via London, and after a sojourn in the US they all sailed across the Atlantic, Kipling continuing his wooing of Caroline on board ship. Caroline was described by Trix as 'plump and plain and on the surface with none of her sister's charm' a 'snub-nosed girl with a cottage loaf figure', though Trix is no impartial witness where her brother's girlfriends were concerned.[69] Her great attraction was doubtless that she was Ted's sister and though Ted was unobtainable, Caroline was not, which made this romance a complex emotional experience for Kipling who was far from getting over Flo Garrard.

They arrived in Liverpool on 5 October 1889 but in less than three weeks time the Hills left for India, recreating in reverse Kipling's previous emotional distancing seven years earlier: where he had travelled to India and left Flo in London in an uncertain state of engagement, now he stayed in London and his fiancée went to India.

Ted had written in her diary 'Carrie engaged to RK' on 9 October, but there was no talk of actual marriage.[70]

Religious differences were raised by Caroline, whose family's strict Protestantism led them to view other denominations with suspicion. Kipling was obliged to write on 9 December 1889 to calm her fears, *Your slave, may he be your sacrifice, was baptised in Bombay Cathedral into the Church of England which you call Episcopalian ... Does that satisfy, dear, that I am not a veiled adherent of the Church of Rome?* [71]

Whether for religious reasons, distance or the evident lack of romance, the relationship had foundered by February when Kipling next saw his sister. Trix later remarked that Kipling told her he had *broken the heart of the noblest woman in the world.*[72] Kipling still seemed to be an adolescent toying with romance.

Plain Tales from the Hills had been published in London in January 1888 and had given Kipling a reputation among the literary set. Andrew Lang remarked that the first appearance of the stories in India was giving the expatriate English readers what they already knew and familiarity dulled their awareness. 'But Mr Kipling's volumes no sooner reached England than the people into whose hands they fell were certain that here were the beginnings of a new literary force. The books had the strangeness, the colour, the variety, the perfume of the East.'[73]

Although Kipling was known and his work eagerly

anticipated by some, money had been spent on his seven months of travelling while little had been made: the proceeds of *From Sea to Sea* as published in instalments in the *Pioneer* in India were slow to arrive. The young writer quickly made the acquaintance of Lang, a significant critic who had responded so positively to *Plain Tales* and had reviewed the *Indian Railway Library* in their Indian editions. Lang was a reader for the publisher Sampson Low and he introduced the publishers to Kipling, who himself negotiated the deal to print the six volumes of stories in Britain which became the means by which Kipling's work became known to a wider reading public. His style was soon so famous it was recognisable in parody: 'This is not a tale. It is a conversation which I had with a complete stranger. If you ask me why I talked to him, I have no very good reason to give. I would simply tell you to spend three hours of solitude in that same compartment on that same line. You may not know the line; which is neither your loss nor the company's gain. I do, and I had spent three hours alone in it; and at the end of three hours I longed for human conversation; I was ready to talk to anyone about anything; I would have talked to a pariah dog; talked kindly too.'[74]

He refused an offer of a permanent job at *St James's Gazette* (*Catch me putting my head into that old noose again*) but was pleased that other magazines, including the *Spectator, Longman's* and *Punch* had asked if he would write for them. He wisely declared he did not come to England to write himself out, *a man can fritter himself away on piece work and be only but a little the richer for it.*[75] He declared his intention to go slowly and do only sufficient magazine work to keep him going while he turned his attention to more substantial fare.

He made a deal with Macmillan to take his writing in return for a retainer, and stories and poems began to appear at regular intervals, including *The Courting of Dinah Shadd*, *On Greenbrow Hill* and *Without Benefit of Clergy*, all of them tales of damaged or distorted love, and clearly part of Kipling's working out of the pain and confusion caused by his flirtation, engagement and abandonment of Caroline Taylor.

In early 1890 the intensity of work and Kipling's miserable personal life got to him and he took an enforced rest. As he wrote to Ted Hill, *My head has given out and I am forbidden work and I am to go away somewhere*.[76] It was not the first nor the last time that nervous exhaustion forced him to stop his punishing self-imposed work schedule.

Hearties and decadents

In December 1889, Macmillan published 'The Ballad of East and West', which immediately established Kipling as a leading poet. Even Tennyson, the Poet Laureate who was soon to die, recognised Kipling as the only one of the younger generation with 'divine fire'.[77] Kipling's verse appealed to the vast, literate public who were not catered for by literary fiction but were above popular romance. It was still, however, usually more sophisticated than is credited by the usual quotation. *East is East and West is West and never the twain shall meet* is a line followed by *But ...* and then describes how the bond between *two strong men* of courage and integrity is forged despite the accidents of race and birth. Like much of Kipling's work, it has been subject to selective quotation and under-reading.

It may be that Kipling had a poor idea of his own worth as a poet. His friend C F Hooper reported Kipling's opinion that 'poetry was a useful means of expressing forceful ideas where they could not be so expressed in prose. His method, as he told the writer many times, was to get a tune in his head and fit words to it.'[78]

Lang introduced Kipling to the Savile Club, a meeting place for literary types where he met such luminaries as Thomas Hardy and Walter Besant. The literary world of London seemed wide open to Kipling but he chose his friends carefully, gravitating towards the conservative and the established rather than the avant garde. He wrote a skit which included the lines,

> I consort with long-haired things
> In velvet collar rolls,
> Who talk about the Aims of Art,
> And 'theories' and 'goals',
> And moo and coo with womenfolk
> About their blessed souls.

He was apparently not tempted by the Wilde crowd, despite his family connections with the Pre-Raphaelites who had led to the aesthetes, who evolved into the decadents. Had he stayed in England and gone to university, Kipling might well have moved towards the school of art for art's sake and become a decadent. As it was he did not seek membership of the Rhymers' Club, formed in 1890 by W B Yeats and others to revitalise the art of poetry. While most Rhymers were lyric poets (which was not Kipling's forte) some, including John Davidson, wrote ballads beside which Kipling's work would not have looked out of place.

Despite disdaining this set, Kipling had more in common with his London contemporaries than was obvious to his later critics, who wanted to see him as a counter-point to effete aesthetes. Kipling's longing for Flo as an unobtainable love is not so different from the same sentiments in such Rhymers as Ernest Dowson, W B Yeats and Arthur Symons. Wilde, a visitor to the Rhymers' Club, famously 'feasted with panthers', the renters and blackmailers of London's sexual underworld just as, to the disgust of his colleagues at the club, Kipling used to trawl the nightlife of the Old City of Lahore to gain his own detailed knowledge of opium dens and brothels. Nor was Wilde so averse to the values of Empire as some of his later admirers would like to think. His poem 'Ave Imperatrix' is as rousing a piece of verse patriotism as was ever written, and was the direct inspiration for a schoolboy poem of Kipling's of the same title. Moreover, the decadents did not disparage the Empire, but they felt themselves to be the culmination of imperial ambition, a period of luxurious surfeit at the height of Empire after which decline was inevitable: a recurring theme in Kipling's more thoughtful pieces.

Kipling had taken his influences from the men around him in the United Services College, the Indian army and the colonial civil service, institutions in which there were sterling qualities, but enlightened liberalism was not among them. Kipling's politics first came to public view in the wake of the scandal after the *Times* published letters implicating the Irish nationalist leader Charles Parnell in the Phoenix Park murders. These letters were shown to be forgeries and a judicial inquiry exonerated Parnell. When he read that Parnell's name had been cleared, in a knee-jerk reaction of the most short-sighted conservatism Kipling was infuriated and re-fashioned some lines he had written in India attacking the judiciary.

In 'Cleared' Kipling rails against Irish nationalist MPs for having connections with what would later be called terrorists and concluding *We are not ruled by murderers, but only – by their friends*. It was an ill-advised piece though brilliantly executed with the force of bottled-up hatred pushed through the trochaic rhythm in vivid imagery to give it a thrilling intensity. The disgraced *Times*, unsurprisingly, chose not to print it. Kipling then took it to Frank Harris, who was editor of the *National Review* and an Irishman who knew a little better than the poet the complexities of Irish politics and also declined it. Finally Kipling struck gold when he offered the piece to W E Henley, who printed it in the *National Observer* ('An Imperial Review'). Henley then became the first to publish the colloquial soldier-speak poems of *Barrack-Room Ballads*, starting with 'Danny Deever' in February 1890 when such vigorous verse was alien to Victorian sensibilities. Over this year Kipling was to supply Henley with some of his most unforgettable verses, which show deep sympathy for the common soldier but are also full of respect and affection for native people:

They've taken of his buttons off an' cut his stripes away,
An' they're hangin' Danny Deever in the mornin'

… it's Tommy this an' Tommy that, an' 'Chuck him out,
        the brute!'
But it's 'Saviour of 'is country' when the guns begin to
        shoot;

Walk wide o' the Widow at Windsor
        For 'alf o' Creation she owns:
        We 'ave bought 'er the same with the sword an' the
                flame,
        An' we've salted it down with our bones.

You big black boundin' beggar – for you broke a British
        square!

        Though I've belted you and flayed you,
        By the livin' Gawd that made you,
You're a better man than I am, Gunga Din!

By the old Moulmein Pagoda, lookin' lazy at the sea,
There's a Burma girl a'settin', and I know she thinks o'
        me;

Wilde was still at this time a friend of Henley and
Yeats was welcome in Henley's circles, but literary life
was increasingly polarised and as the nineties progressed, the Hearties or 'Henley's Regatta' came to be the
literary coterie in which Kipling found company. They
included Henry Rider Haggard, whose great works of

imperial adventure, *She* and *King Solomon's Mines*, had been written in the 1880s, so he was already the supreme adventure writer when Kipling met him. Kipling had entered a very male group devoted to the depiction of real or idealised male experiences, in which women were remote figures of romance. He was rather contemptuous of the literary scene generally: the loneliness of his early time in London would have been assuaged had he more freely accepted invitations and acted more generously towards those members of the older generation eager to meet him. Even Henley did not escape Kipling's scorn; he resisted Henley's referring to him as 'one of my young men' and said to Trix, *Henley is a great man; he is also a cripple, but he is not going to come the bullying cripple over me, after I have been in harness all these years.*[79]

Trix said Kipling's success in India was doled out drop by drop, whereas in London it came as a flood. Despite his badtempered remarks, he was not to suffer rejection. Kipling called in to see the editor of *St James's Gazette*, Sidney Low, who had asked to see him after reading some of his stories. Low described him as 'a short, dark, young man with a bowler hat, a rather shabby tweed overcoat, an emphatic voice, a charming smile, and behind his spectacles a pair of the brightest eyes I had ever seen. He told me that he had to make his way in English literature, and intended to do it ...' Kipling agreed to write a piece for the *Gazette*. Low later described him breezing into his office and speaking about a parliamentary Bill that the *Gazette* had supported, intended to stop unscrupulous ship-owners from sending ships to sea in a dangerous condition. *I say,*

Kipling said, *I like those screeds of yours on the coffin-ships. Do you want a poem about them? Low said he did so Kipling said, Give me some paper, something to smoke, and something to drink, and you shall have it.*[80] Kipling's needs were supplied, he was given a room and in just over an hour Low called in to find him with 12 stanzas of 'The Ballad of the Bolivar', about seven sailors who left the Ratcliffe Road in London in a coffin-ship:

> Felt her hog and felt her sag, betted when she'd break;
>> Wondered every time she raced if she'd stand the
>> shock;
> Heard the seas like drunken men pounding at her
> strake;
>> Hoped the Lord 'ud keep His thumb on the
>> plummer-block!

Low was duly impressed, and spoke widely of the young poet's prodigious abilities. Kipling was, of course, showing off. As everyone knew who had observed his working methods closer than Low, Kipling composed poems to a rhythm in his head. A literary visitor wrote, 'his mouth was his pen. That has always been his way, to compose a poem in his head, to get it right and taut, and when it is all done to copy it out on paper in his clear, small handwriting.'[81]

Despite his previous incarnation as a reporter, he could be very stand-offish to journalists unless they passed his test as men of action and he warmed to them. One such was a sailor, Roger Peacock, who interviewed Kipling for *Lloyd's Newspaper* but found, 'Not only had he been interviewing me, but found out more about me in ten minutes than my parents ever knew. So he interviews everybody, getting each man's facts like a fishwife cleaning a herring before he knows it ... He got his knowledge, not by wasting his time in forecastle, camp or barrack, not from school, not as the second-hand stuff one gains from printed books. It was learned at first hand from men. His eyes see one through to the bones, his questions are sharp and deep-searching as a surgeon's knife, and his brain files the facts away in a memory as big as a library.'[82]

The novel that failed

Few English writers in Kipling's time had become famous through writing short stories and none had scaled great heights; the short story was taken as a harbinger of more powerful works to come. Literary London was watching Kipling to see if he would produce a great novel, and Kipling himself had long been aware that he should be writing a long work to pull his talents together.

Kipling had playfully made a point of abandoning *Mother Maturin*, his vast novel of Anglo-Indian life. The last story in *Plain Tales from the Hills* was called 'To Be Filed for Reference'. It deals with the narrator's friendship with McIntosh Jellaludin, an educated Englishman who has gone native and married an Indian woman and become an alcoholic. Before he dies he gives the narrator a bulky manuscript *showing what he saw and how he lived, and what befell him and others; being also an account of the life and sins and death of Mother Maturin*. The narrator edits the manuscript but leaves its possible future publication to fate, yet makes a point of stating that he wrote the story *as a safeguard to prove that McIntosh Jel-laludin and not I myself wrote the Book of Mother Maturin*. After the abandonment of *Mother Maturin* he took another track and was working towards a novel in *The Gadsbys*, a series of self-contained stories adding together to make a greater whole.

A commission is a great spur to further productivity and Kipling was fortunate to be working at the time for *Lippincott's Magazine*, an American publication which combed literary London to buy the work of new, young talent. A lunch in February 1889 between *Lippincott's* agent, Conan Doyle and Oscar Wilde resulted in the magazine commissioning the first of the *Sherlock Holmes* stories and *The Picture of Dorian Gray*, two of the most important works of the 1890s. *Lippincott's*, doubtless in the person of the same agent, then approached Kipling for a long piece. Kipling's friend C F Hooper described how the proviso was 'that the manuscript should be delivered in a week. It was assumed, of course, that he had a long story ready for delivery. Kipling had always been in doubt whether he could last over the "long course". He had nothing at all to suit at the time, but accepted the offer and also the stipulation. Then he worked day and night, finishing the book in four days from receiving the commission. The effort was more than he could stand and he was seriously ill in consequence.'[83]

This account is not literally true, but another example of the way in which the Kipling myth was rounded by retelling among those of his slight acquaintance. He did not work to such an absurd deadline, but still a rather exacting one of three months as he grappled with the most complex problem of his literary life to date in writing *The Light that Failed.*

Kipling laboured under the internal pressure of his professional need to produce a long work; a deadline; and the emotional charge resulting from the way in which a book of some autobiographical complexity was being written while the story it reflected was being played out in his life. The spark that lit *The Light that Failed* was the reappearance in Kipling's life of Flo Garrard.

The young writer was often depressed in his first weeks alone in London; *There are five million people in London this night, and saving those who starve, I don't think there is one more heartsick or thoroughly wretched than that 'rising young author' known to you as: Ruddy*, he wrote.[84] On some lonely wandering in the London fog on the embankment of the Thames in late January or early February 1890 he met Flo. As he described it in the novel, *There was no mistaking. The years had turned the child to a woman, but they had not altered the dark-grey eyes, the thin scarlet lips, or the firmly-modelled mouth and chin; and, that all should be as it was of old, she wore a closely fitting grey dress.*[85]

Trix visited Kipling on 11 February 1890, shortly after this meeting, and was able to recount that her brother 'was instantly her slave again'. 'She refused him more than once – his love took a deal of killing – and I think she half accepted him, or he thought she did.'[86]

When Kipling met Flo again she had finished at the

Slade School and was due to study further at the Académie Julian in Paris. In the novel the Flo character Maisie's half-hearted acceptance of Kipling (in the character of Dick) extends to permitting him to visit her on Sunday afternoons and seeking his advice on her work. For Kipling the visits to Flo took place but not the constructive criticism – Kipling had no great skill in her field. An extant sketchbook of Flo's shows Kipling's lively stick-cartoons giving a jocular commentary on Flo – such drolleries as accidentally starting a fire with her cigarette; and running from a bull when she tries to paint in a field.

Trix said Flo was 'naturally cold – her very face and magnoliapetal complexion showed that – and she wanted to live her own life and paint her very ineffective little pictures.'[87] This is certainly the impression Maisie gives to Dick in the novel, for she shows considerable self-knowledge, when she thinks of herself as being selfish because she is using Dick's skills while she is unable to give him the love he craves in return. Dick is completely unable to conceive *that Maisie should refuse sooner or later to love him, since he loved her*.[88] He feels that his success should command love. He has been brave, and deserves the fair, but finds the fair has her own interests.

Kipling visited Flo at her house in London where she was living with Mabel Price, three years older than her and the daughter of an Oxford Mathematics don. Mabel had studied at the Slade in Oxford and later in London before going to the Académie Julian with Flo. In *The Light that Failed* Maisie is living with a 'red haired girl' who is not named and whose relationship with Maisie is indistinct except that she has power over her and seems to despise Dick. She is furious, for example, when Maisie permits Dick a chaste kiss when the two women go off together to France.

Flo's indifference to him, her resistance to the display of his abilities, probed a deep wound of loneliness and rejection in Kipling. His parents had abandoned him in the House of Desolation with no justification that was comprehensible to him; now he could not make the girl he loved love him back. Kipling, irresistibly drawn back to past failures, tried again. Again, Trix remarked that she did not think that Flo 'did anything to kill his love; she was simply not attracted by anything he had to offer.'[89]

Kipling visited Flo in Paris from 24 to 28 May 1890, where she was living with Mabel Price in the Avenue de Jena. Little is known about this time except that they went to the countryside to sketch and to picnic with friends. Kipling must have manoeuvred the time to allow him some private moments of conversation with Flo for he was never to see her again, and clearly something had transpired between them that ended the relationship and sent Kipling off in a white heat of furious creativity.

If she had not found it before, now Flo had definitely discovered her sexual orientation. It is not known whether she told Kipling she was a lesbian; or he worked it out for himself on seeing her intimacy with Mabel; or perhaps never did understand explicitly, except that she rejected his advances and gave him no hope for the future.

Soon after his return he wrote *The Light that Failed*, with a theme drawn from Elizabeth Barrett Browning's *Aurora Leigh* but with strongly autobiographical elements. The book begins with Maisie and Dick, recognisably Kipling and Flo, on a seashore playing with a revolver. They are children *companions in bondage* boarding in a place familiar as the House of Desolation from 'Baa Baa Black Sheep'. Maisie, a *long-haired, grey-eyed little atom* with a pet goat, as had Flo, stood up to the Mrs Holloway character and earned Dick's lasting respect. The game on the beach ends in Maisie accidentally discharging the revolver near Dick's face, an event which is probably the ultimate cause of his blindness (though other causes are given when it is diagnosed). In the same place, Maisie is talking about her imminent departure from the boarding house and Dick declares his feelings for her and coaxes a kiss for the first time.

Dick is then seen as a young man in the Sudan campaign, with the camaraderie of masculine company. He is a war artist, demonstrating the possibility of being both creative and a man of action and full of *the austere love that springs up between men who have tugged the same oar together*.[90]

The slaughter of Gordon and the loss of the Sudan to what were considered savages in 1884 was a wound to the British Empire that would have to be treated. While Kipling was writing this was a burning political issue which was to continue through most of the decade: Kitchener was not ordered to begin the reconquest of the Sudan, a key element of Kipling's plot, until 1896, six years after the first publication of *The Light that Failed*, though expeditionary skirmishes on the Sudanese border continued throughout.

Dick goes to London where his pictures are attracting attention, and he suffers on a diet of sausage and mash. He meets Maisie in the fog on the Embankment and against his will, *every pulse of Dick's body throbbed furiously and his palate dried in his mouth.*[91] He walks beside her and they have a desultory conversation. She has also become an artist, studying in London and France. She tells him she works in the park but doesn't give him her address, and catches her bus. It was, as it must have been for Kipling, a meeting in which all the affection was on one side, and the woman was merely mildly interested to see him again.

He sees her again and tells her his story, *the I – I – I's flashing through the records as telegraph-poles fly past the traveller.*[92] In Kipling's view, if he is a dedicated and successful creative artist, the woman he desires *should* love him. For Flo this was not enough but for Kipling's character Dick, the object of his affections is only too impressed by his success. Dick takes her to a print ship where people are admiring his work in the window and the fiercely ambitious Maisie envies his fame. Maisie's is a tale of *patient toil backed by savage pride* where she struggles on with no success. He declares love but she is dedicated to her work and wants only his advice.

Maisie goes off to France with the red-haired girl. Dick's friend Torpenhow becomes entangled with a prostitute, Bessie, who he helps when he finds her collapsed with hunger; Dick earns her enmity by sending Torpenhow away when she is about to move in with him. Dick finds he is losing his sight and he uses Bessie as a model for his last great picture, of Melancholia, the subject Maisie said she was going off to France to paint. Under the pretext of cleaning up, Bessie destroys the masterpiece. Dick has gone blind before he finds out about the destruction and Torpenhow, out of pity for his disabled friend, does not enlighten him. *Torpenhow thrust out a large and hairy paw from the long chair. Dick clutched it tightly, and in half an hour had fallen asleep. Torpenhow withdrew his hand and, stooping over Dick, kissed him lightly on the forehead, as men do sometimes kiss a wounded comrade in the hour of death, to ease his departure.*[93]

Torpenhow goes to France to bring Maisie to Dick, but after seeing him blindly displaying his ruined picture, she runs out. Maisie is last seen alone in her house in London, ashamed of herself for her treatment of Dick but unable to change; neither a great painter nor a great lover and therefore a failure both as an artist and a woman.

Torpenhow and others go off to join in the reconquest of the Sudan, leaving Dick alone in his rooms. While out walking with his landlord, Dick encounters Bessie and she returns to his rooms and soon tells him that she ruined his picture. He determines on a last great gesture. He travels to the army via Egypt and reacquaints himself with the terrain and the army, being shot dead at last as he reaches his beloved friend.

The strain of creation under such emotional burdens as Kipling faced saw him overload the plot with implausibilities which show Kipling shrinking in the face of what he had created. He is simply unable to face Maisie's (and therefore Flo's) lesbian relationship, and therefore has the red-haired girl confessing love for Dick. Mabel Price made a point of telling Kipling's official biographer that no such thing had happened, so clearly did she see herself in the picture of the red-haired girl.[94] Kipling wants the love between men to be noble, pure and untainted by sex with women so the reader is expected to believe Torpenhow would rather leave the country at Dick's bidding than have sex with a willing girl. Finally, there is no way such a noble man as Dick would appear on the battlefield in an enfeebled state which would endanger his comrades by obliging them to care for him.

On the other hand, the figure of the heroic but wounded imperialist riding literally blindly into another desert adventure where he will certainly die is one which could only have been created by Kipling the great poet of Empire. Dick's life and fatal last ride is also a metaphor for the failing gallantry of nineteenth-century man confronting the new woman, which makes it a richer and more interesting story than many contemporaries realised. It has remained in print and is now a classic text in gender studies, used to examine the pathological inability of men such as Kipling to accept the new woman, and to be mined for its homoerotic undercurrents.

The man-loving and misogynistic nature of the book was not lost on contemporary writers. Max Beerbohm slyly remarks that with its adoration of military men, if we knew only this work of Kipling's, we should assure it was the pen name of a woman writer; 'strange that these heroes with their self-conscious blurting of oaths and slang, their cheap cynicism about the female sex, were not fondly created out of the inner consciousness of a female novelist.'[95]

As usual, Kipling had wrought his experiences into art: his terror of blindness (a genuine and realistic fear for him given his history of poor sight); but is also an age-old symbol of sexual impotence and thus taken to symbolise both his loss of creative power and the surrender of the male force to female will.

The light is the light of his eyes but also the light of female love which is betrayed when Flo and Maisie take up a man's instruments: the smoking gun and the smoking cigarette are both masculine symbols which a woman can hold but in Kipling's ideal world, should not. Tobacco is taken as a symbol of male bonding: *Have you any tobacco?* being an effective password to male intimacy. Dick goes *whistling to his chambers with a strong yearning for some man-talk and tobacco after his first experience of an entire day spent in the society of a woman.*[96]

Maisie is recognisably a type who recurs in English novels of the 1890s. Her only obvious precursor was in Kipling's friend Rider Haggard's adventure *She* (1887). Kipling's work was to be followed by Du Maurier's *Trilby* (1894), Grant Allen's *The Woman Who Did* (1895) and Thomas Hardy's *Jude the Obscure* (1895), all with similarly maddening, self-directed, desirable yet distant modern women.

The storyline of *The Light that Failed* given here is as published by Macmillan in March 1891. The first version, published in the USA in November 1890, was shorter, having 12 chapters not 15, and had an improbable happy ending with the engagement of Maisie and Dick. The new version had a brief note from Kipling that it was *the story of The Light that Failed as it was originally conceived by the Writer* which suggests that the ending was a change advised by *Lippincott's* (though Kipling's friend Wolcott Balestier has also been suggested as the one who advised on a happy ending). Kipling, however, was quite capable of varied meanings in these personal addresses to the audience and it may be that he wrote and rewrote a generally unsatisfactory book with no urging from publishers, just as he subsequently made further, minor revisions. The first full version was dedicated to his mother.

The pressure of his doomed relationship with Flo combined with his routine of work and his intense loneliness to send Kipling into a nervous breakdown. There is little record of this. Very few letters survive from the period of 1890 when Kipling was seeing Flo again, writing *The Light that Failed* and suffering his breakdown; and none refer to these events except a letter to a young correspondent: *I am nearly broked in two. I have done my two books an' I'm dead tired and frabjous an' muzzy about the head.*[97] By common consent, Kipling finished *The Light that Failed* in August, suffered a breakdown in September and recuperated in Italy at the Naples home of Lord Dufferin, the former viceroy and now a family friend, in October 1890.

His novel is the only lengthy clue to what was happening to Kipling: the way Dick was *feeling* like a limp-wristed decadent but acting like a muscular hearty is a biographical pointer to the dichotomy Kipling was experiencing in London in the brilliant 1890s.

On publication, critical voices were not kind to Kipling who had so startled them with short stories which they had praised but reserved judgement on his writing, thinking his stories to be the precursor of his real work, a great novel. Mrs Oliphant found it unputdownable and read it all night but others were not impressed. Henry James, previously Kipling's biggest fan, called it 'the most youthfully infirm of his productions'.[98] The influential critic Edmund Gosse said 'with its extremely disagreeable woman, and its far more brutal; and detestable man … I confess that it is *The Light that Failed* that has wakened me to the fact that there are limits to this dazzling new talent'[99] *The Bookman* said 'His fresh start, *The Light that Failed*, was a false one … He may strengthen, but cannot alter his place in literature. That place is not beside the great masters of imperishable fiction … '[100]

Kipling showed the same disdain for their negative as he had for their positive criticism, though it is as well he never saw what Flo Garrard wrote. She continued to live with women and paint pictures, and on the flyleaf of her copy of the book, signing herself Maisie, she wrote 'If you happen to read this singular, if somewhat murky little story you are very likely to rather wonder if real people could be quite so stupid and objectionable as this crowd.

'Of course its difficult to see oneself as others see you, still m'thinks there's something somewhat distorted about it all; and that the story does not run its entire length on lines quite parallel with Truth.

'It looks to me rather like its image reflected in a

Distorting Mirror appearing all distorted, and grotesque.'[101]

The only addition to the story of Flo Garrard in Kipling's life is that he went on to kill her. That is, he said to Trix in 1902 *Do you remember Flo?*

'Of course, I shall never forget her.'

Well she died three months ago: neglected lungs I think, she never took the least care of herself.[102]

It is quite possible that Kipling had made a mistake (or Trix had) but far more likely that he decided to fictionalise her death, just as he fictionalised her life. By killing her he could lose that troublesome part of his memory, of romantic and literary failure. In fact she became a painter of portraits and landscapes, exhibited regularly in the Paris Salon and once had a small exhibition in Bond Street. She died two years after Kipling on 31 January 1938 at the age of 73, attended by the partner of her later years, Frances Egerton. Her obituarist still thought it necessary to remark on 'Miss Garrard's sturdy figure and rather masculine costume.'[103]

A Home in America

Towards the end of 1890 an event occurred that might have changed the course of Kipling's life and it is worth pondering precisely because it did not change him. Professor Aleck Hill died suddenly in India on 23 September. While the grief of a family to which he had been close would affect Kipling, it would be impossible for him not to note that now the beloved Edmonia – Ted – Hill was available and able to marry a young man who had chastely paid court to her in all the years of their acquaintance.

When Ted and her sister Caroline passed through London on their way back to America in December, they saw Kipling at least twice, when he called on them at the Hotel Metropole, but his relationship with Ted did not take off, and it was nine years before they resumed even a warm exchange of letters. When love was available to be grasped, Kipling turned away from it.

However, Kipling's friendship with the Hills in India had started a long and beneficial relationship with the United States, both in personal and professional terms. In addition to *The Light that Failed*, two books were published in America in spring 1891: an authorised book called *Mine Own People* and a collection of stories collected from various magazines by Harpers and published as *The Courting of Dinah Shadd and Other Stories*. Kipling was furious at the latter as he had not been consulted, or permitted to revise the stories, and had negotiated no payment. In an insulting aside they sent him a £10 note as recompense.

He was enraged not only that his work should be thus taken, but that it should be done by Harpers who had sent him on his way with a cursory rejection when he had called on them in New York and offered his stories. He stormed in the literary magazine *The Athenaeum: Messrs Harper & Brothers appropriated my tales without asking my permission, had not the courtesy to allow me to revise proofs before jamming those tales into a job-work volume, and sent me a ten pound note as notification of outrage perpetrated.*[104]

Harpers' defence was that Kipling was ungracious: they had fairly bought serial (though not book) rights and other publishers would just have appropriated the stories without even sending Kipling the £10. Kipling resentfully acknowledged this – the real problem was the unprofessional state of copyright law between the US and UK which meant any work could be pirated. This was a wretched set of affairs that had long needed resolution. A sterling attempt was made by Wolcott Balestier, British agent for the US firm of Lovell, who set out to make payments to authors in order to create goodwill in this murky situation. The rewards of magnanimous behaviour now, it was believed, would be garnered in the future when the inevitable international copyright agreement would be imposed on the pirates.

He had, for example, published *The Light that Failed* in book form in the US a few days before its magazine publication (by *Lippincott's*) in order to establish precedence; and organised an 'Authorised Version' of Kipling's stories for the US market which would hopefully undercut the pirates.

Balestier, four years older than Kipling and living in London only a little longer, was a man of prodigious energy and charm who was quickly to become friends not only with Kipling but with Henry James, Edmund Gosse, George Meredith, Mrs Humphrey Ward and other literary leading lights of the day.

Hailing from Brattleboro, Vermont, he was educated at Cornell University, and trained as a journalist before working in publishing, though he always wanted to be a writer and had written three short novels. Probably in summer 1890, he and Kipling discussed an adventure story set in America and India and resolved to write a novel in collaboration. They were deep into the work by February 1891, Balestier mainly writing the first four chapters, which were set in the American West, while Kipling concentrated on the following chapters in India.

A critic in Vermont who presumably had first-hand information from the family, described their methods: 'the work was done by the two friends – Balestier who is an accomplished typewriter, sitting at the machine and dashing off the sentences and chapters while Kipling paced the room, each composing, suggesting, or criticising in turn, and the mind of each stimulating the other to its best work.'[105]

The Naulahka is another working of some of the themes from *The Light that Failed*, with the hero, American engineer Nicholas Tarvin, enjoying adventures while the heroine, missionary Kate Sheriff, has to choose whether to renounce her career for marriage. Tarvin's life's work is to bring the railway to his small Colorado town while Kate learns of the sufferings of Indian women and trains as a nurse to work with them. Subtitled as 'A story of West and East', it is an adventure story with the exotic settings of the American west and princely India. The Naulahka is a necklace of legendary beauty which is the object of a subplot that brings Nicholas to India, whence Kate has preceded him. It is taken as an indication of Kipling's affection for Balestier, who had control of the setting and publication of the story while Kipling was travelling, that he tolerated his friend's misspelling of the Indian word Naulakha and allowed both serial and book publication with the wrong spelling once Balestier had made the mistake. Kipling spelled the word correctly in his letters.

As is clear from Kipling's willingness to collaborate with Balestier, his influence on Kipling was profound, though little written evidence remains of their relationship, which gives the editor of Kipling's letters to believe that it was deliberately destroyed. It may have been, however, that they spent so much time together that letters were superfluous. Balestier's sister Josephine wrote home, 'After the authors' dinner the other night Wolcott and young Kipling talked until four in the morning. They are growing fast friends; they are very congenial, dove-tail finely. I think it rather picturesque that the two London literary infants should play so prettily together.'[106]

A later friend, the American novelist, academic and

sometime secretary to Mark Twain, Charles Stoddard, said Balestier had 'found and nourished [Kipling's] fainting spirit. Perhaps there never was a more beautiful friendship than theirs, or a sadder one.'[107] Kipling found in Wolcott Balestier a friend as close as any family member, his best friend. There has been conjecture that they had a physical relationship. Not only is there no explicit evidence for this but, implicitly, it is unlikely in the extreme as it would go against all known facts about the sexual behaviour of Kipling and (rather more importantly) his literary behaviour: such an important event in his life would have been reflected in his work had it taken place.

With his family together, Kipling's 25th birthday party in December 1890 was a celebration of hardships endured and overcome, of the young man crowned with laurels. His parents Lockwood and Alice Kipling had returned from India temporarily and now lived in the Earls Court Road with Trix and her husband, so the family square was again united when Kipling visited, which he did increasingly often. Other members of the Balestier family also joined Wolcott in London and it was natural for the two families to meet. The Balestiers included his younger sister Caroline, a small, plain woman three years older than Kipling with a strong sense of determination and organisation. It was these supposedly masculine qualities that led Lockwood Kipling to call her 'a good man spoiled'. Alice Kipling with her usual quick-witted intuition said: 'That woman is going to marry our Ruddy' and was reported to be unenthusiastic about the prospect.[108] There was said to be an understanding between Kipling and Carrie Balestier before he left London for a world tour in August 1891.

Kipling's call to imperial service, 'The English Flag', was published in April 1891 and was almost immediately given pride of place in Henley's anthology of verse *Lyra Heroica*, which quickly became the most popular collection of verse for children, particularly as it was often given as a prize to stimulate imperial responsibility. It was by this means, and by his later stories for children, that Kipling began to conquer a new generation of readers.

Kipling felt he had poured a great deal into his work and needed his usual panacea, which was travel. He may also have been heeding warnings from those who felt he was writing himself out and needed a new intake of exotic experiences. He therefore set off for South Africa, then called at Australia and New Zealand. He was in India with his parents, who had returned to Lahore, when he received a telegram from Caroline Balestier saying that her brother was dead.

Wolcott had gone to Germany on business and had died of typhoid in Dresden on 6 December; it was believed that he had been ill when he left London and had travelled despite his infection. His mother and sisters, visiting Paris, had been contacted by a business partner and had hastened to be present at Wolcott's bed. He was buried in Germany with his mother and sisters present, but only Henry James of his literary friends. James drove back from the cemetery with Carrie, describing her as 'remarkable in her force, acuteness, capacity and courage – and in the intense – almost manly nature of her emotion. She is a worthy sister of poor dear big-spirited, only-by-death-quenched Wolcott.'[109]

Kipling returned to England, seeing Carrie in London on 10 January 1892. Probably at this meeting they agreed to be married, and took out a special licence the following day so the ceremony could be conducted in just over a week. The wedding took place at All Soul's, Langham Place. Few were told and fewer still came: London was in the grip of a flu epidemic affecting all the members of Carrie's family who were in the city and most of Kipling's. Only Kipling's cousin Ambrose (always known as Ambro') Poynter was present from his family, and literary friends Edmund Gosse and William Heinemann (with whom Wolcott had been in a business relationship). Henry James gave away the bride without much evident joy, he wrote to his brother, '[she] is a hard devoted capable little person whom I don't in the least understand his marrying. It is a union of which I don't forecast the future though I gave her away in a dreary little wedding with an attendance simply of four men.'[110]

Why did he marry Carrie, and why so fast? The family story is that before he died Wolcott charged Kipling with the care of his family. This is very likely: he was head of the family as Mrs Balestier was a widow; and his younger brother Beatty was not a man to be relied upon. Whether in a delirium of fever or not, the dying man would certainly have feared for the future of his loved ones and could well have suggested his successful friend Kipling as their guardian. Family tradition also has it that Carrie and Kipling were close to being engaged before Kipling's departure so marriage was not altogether a surprise.

Doubtless in the weeks of bereavement the thought of planning for a large society wedding later in the year was more than they could bear and, having decided to do it, the couple felt they might as well do it fast.

The groom described the conflicting emotions he felt in letters to his aunt Louisa Baldwin and to his old headmaster Cormell Price: *I am riotously happy* but *we have gone through deep waters together ... this is inexpressibly awful and I ought to feel bad but I am in a state of sinful joy.*[111]

Kipling was a literary lion and could easily have had a pretty young 'trophy' wife. That he did not is testament to his recognition that he needed a strong, capable woman, that all those he had loved in the past, including his mother, were in this mould. There was also his shock at losing his friend and perhaps a feeling that making a commitment of his life to Balestier's family was the finest thing he could do. As it turned out, marriage to Carrie Balestier was the best emotional decision of Kipling's life, giving him an intelligent companion, mother to three children, a capable business manager and a protector from the intrusions of the world.

Going west

Carrie, who had been her brother's office manager, now wound up his business affairs. Kipling was eager to leave London and doubtless Carrie too felt miserable in a city she associated with her brother. Kipling had £2,000 in his bank account and there was no reason the couple should not go off on a world trip. Their first port of call was to the Balestier family home, to which Mrs Balestier and sister Josephine accompanied them in sailing from Liverpool for New York.

Before he left, Kipling published *Barrack-Room Ballads*, a collection of his soldier and empire poems, many of which had previously appeared in Henley's *National Observer*. The first collection of mature verse from Kipling available to the English public, it was an immediate best-seller, running through three editions and selling 7,000 copies in the first year.

He dedicated the volume to Wolcott Balestier and on his journey across the Atlantic completed *The Naulahka*, which was lacking one or more of its nine instalments. It was already being serialised monthly in the *Century Magazine*, leaving Kipling the painful task of completing alone the work conceived jointly with his friend. It is charitable to think it was the difficult circumstances of writing which led to the crude execution of the book's ending. It had always been part of the plan to have Kate see the error of her manner of thinking and settle down to marriage with Nicholas, but Kipling's rendering of her total capitulation is not credible:

'It was a mistake' she said.

'What?'

'Everything. My coming. My thinking I could do it. It's not a girl's work. It's my work, perhaps; but it's not for me. I have given it up, Nick. Take me home.'

Later she reflects on her surrender to gender type, *In that hour, luxuriously disposed upon many cushions, she realised nothing more than a woman's complete contentment with the fact that there was a man in the world to do things for her.*[112]

The Kipling family group went by train to Vermont where they alighted to a North American winter, *Thirty below freezing!* Kipling wrote. *It was inconceivable until one stepped out into it at midnight, and the first shock of that clear, still air took away the breath as a plunge into sea water does. A walrus sitting on a woolpack [Beatty Balestier] was our host in his sleigh, and he wrapped us in hairy goatskin coats, caps that came down over the ears, buffalo robes and blankets, and yet more buffalo-robes, till we, too, looked like walruses and moved almost as gracefully.*[113]

Kipling found the climate and the scenery entrancing and he decided with his bride that they would build a house on some of the Balestier land at Brattleboro, within sight of Mount Monadnock. Beatty Balestier gave them about ten acres of his farm in return for $750, retaining pasture and some other rights.

The couple now proceeded on their honeymoon: west to Chicago, Winnipeg and Vancouver and off to Japan. From April to June they were in Yokohama, where Kipling used the local branch of the Oriental Banking Company. He called in one morning to collect a small amount of cash and the manager suggested he take some more. Kipling did not take the hint; when he called back that afternoon the door was locked: the bank had collapsed, and with it the entire proceeds of Kipling's labours.

The couple's assets were now a return ticket to Vancouver and $100 in a New York bank. To contribute to their change in fortunes, Carrie must have been certain by now that she was pregnant. Kipling said, *There was an instant Committee of Ways and Means, which advanced our* understanding of each other more than a cycle of solvent matrimony.[114] They cancelled the forward advance of their honeymoon and Kipling's celebrity doubtless eased the refund from Thomas Cook of their cancelled reservations. They therefore had some ready money and stayed in Japan before making the trip home. Kipling was a man who found petty obstacles harder to confront than great ones, and he sailed through this disaster with a dignity he found himself unable to muster when faced, for example, with questions from reporters, which always made him querulous.

They were back in Vermont by late July 1892, staying with Beatty Balestier and appealing to Carrie's wealthy grandmother for help. She gave them Bliss Cottage, a labourer's house on the estate. It was a severe test of character: Kipling's fortune was all but wiped out, and now he with his heavily pregnant wife were living in a labourer's cottage miles from anywhere with the additional responsibility of Wolcott's family to look out for. He had little time for writing in the first year, when he had to work to make the house weatherproof before the severe winter, but Bliss Cottage lived up to its name. As he described it: When winter shut down and sleigh-bells rang all over the white world that tucked us in, we counted ourselves secure. Sometimes we had a servant. Sometimes she would find the solitude too much for her and flee without warning, one even leaving her trunk ...When our lead pipe froze, we would slip on our coon-skin coats and thaw it out with a lighted candle. There was no space in the bedroom for a cradle, so we decided that a trunk-tray would be just as good. We envied no one – not even when skunks wandered into our cellar and, knowing the nature of the beasts, we immobilised ourselves till it should please them to depart.[115]

Kipling's neighbours found something odd about their new acquaintance, who was reported to make as much as a hundred dollars out of a ten-cent bottle of ink but it was as well that Kipling could make more money.[116] He was borne out by the arrival of royalties for The Naulahka and Barrack-Room Ballads, which started at $150 in September but rose to $3,888 in November.

The couple had already been planning the house they wanted to have built on the land they had bought from Beatty, which they had designed by a New York architect to their specifications. They called it Naulakha (spelling the name correctly, as it had not been in the title of the novel), which is an indication of the importance of the novel to Kipling and of the fact that it was the advance on the book that paid for the land. The name was also a coded reference to Wolcott, coded because Kipling would not allow his name to be mentioned and no photographs of him were permitted in the house, so painful did he find the memory of his lost friend. A link to Wolcott was also necessarily a token of his bond to Carrie. The Naulahka had also been the novel in which Flo/Maisie, in the person of Kate Sheriff, finally capitulated and submitted herself and her career to male will, giving Kipling a completion of that part of his life.

Beatty acted as agent for the building of Naulakha, taking a commission on the work which was paid for by Carrie in small sums. She liked to keep control over Beatty, the youngest of four Balestier children, who had been a spoiled child and had never really grown up. In the early years relations were good between the Kiplings and their near neighbours Beatty and his wife Mai, who gave country parties with home-brewed cider and a fiddler for entertainment. Kipling wrote to friends that he had sunshine and peace of mind.

Kipling did his best around the house but he was completely incompetent at anything technical – even putting screens on windows would defeat him. This makes his virtuosity in describing technical terms in his writing all the more remarkable. It was in Vermont that he wrote the finest of these, 'McAndrew's Hymn', the Scots engineer's consecration of his machine to the Almighty:

> From coupler-flange to spindle-guide I see Thy Hand, O
> God –
> Predestination in the stride o' yon connectin'-rod.

Kipling was paid $500 for the poem by *Scribner's Magazine*, an American record. Kipling became entranced by the notion of machinery talking to itself and later wrote 'The Ship that Found Herself' about a ship discovering her 'soul' on a trans-Atlantic maiden voyage, and the similar '.007' about a train.

The Kiplings' first child was born at Bliss Cottage on 29 December 1892. As Kipling's birthday was on the 30th and Carrie's on 31 December, he remarked *we congratulated her on her sense of the fitness of things, and she throve in her trunk-tray in the sunshine on the little plank veranda.*[117] They called her Josephine, after Carrie's younger sister.

The Kiplings moved into Naulakha in late summer 1893; the house had cost them $11,000. Carrie ran the household with a determined and rather austere hand. She liked to have her own way and once lost both of her servants over a triviality: the cook because she refused to wear a cap, which was part of the uniform Carrie ordained, and the maid who left in sympathy with the cook. Kipling worked in his study from nine to one each day while Carrie sat in an anteroom outside with her account books and needlework, forbidding anyone entrance to the master's study.

Over the years they were there Kipling's old friend from the *Civil and Military Gazette* Kay Robinson visited, as did Conan Doyle and Lockwood Kipling, but space for guests was limited and the couple normally enjoyed the early years of their married life alone. Kipling confided to Carrie, and she wrote in her diary, that he had the 'return of a feeling of great strength, such as he had when he first came to London and met the men he was pitted against.'[118] This vigour, a high point in his creative life, coincided with his joy at having his own home, wife and child.

Josephine in particular gave him endless delight. Though Kipling could be difficult with adults, he never was with children, who could always command his attention. Josephine, called Joss, was a charming child with large blue eyes and fair hair. Kipling used to write delightful letters in her name when relatives gave her presents: *I want to thank you for my White Seal slippers. They are good to eat though hairy ...*[119]

Kipling would tell her stories at night and she would

be found repeating them to her dolls the next morning. She quickly became the equal of her cousin, Beatty and Mai's child, who was two years older than her. As she grew, while Kipling was working and she knew he could not be disturbed, she would approach him silently and put her hand in his.

In his creative life it was as if having children had opened a spring flowing with narrative. Part of this was the creation of fictional children, but they were not the sickening children of Victorian fiction. His most sympathetic characters, Kim and Mowgli, were resourceful orphans; Harvey in *Captains Courageous* becomes an orphan for his voyage; and Kipling frequently returned to the theme of children in an adult world as he had in 'Wee Willie Winkie' and 'Tods' Amendment', in both of which the child shows superior wisdom. Six was a frequent age for Kipling's child characters – the age he was when he was left in the House of Desolation.

At his time of his greatest happiness, in the early years in Vermont, it was as if he was working out the suffering of childhood by rewriting it, something he did with the little-known story 'The Potted Princess' of summer 1892. Two children, the Punch and Judy from 'Baa Baa Black Sheep', are not sent to the House of Desolation in England but stay in India with their devoted parents, surrounded by adoring servants and speaking Hindustani *because they understood it better than English*.[120] While children had often occurred in his writing, in the books following Josephine's birth children and stories for children predominated. *Kim, Captains Courageous, Stalky & Co* and the two *Jungle Books* have children as central characters, while *Just So Stories, Puck of Pook's Hill* and *Rewards and Fairies* were written for children.

In November 1892 while still at Bliss Cottage, he was writing 'a wolf-story' called 'Mowgli's Brothers' for the *St Nicholas Magazine* with a character called Mowgli who was raised by wolves. Before this was published a Mowgli story written later, 'In the Rukh', with Mowgli as a grown man looking back over his life, came out in the book of stories *Many Inventions*. Mowgli stories continued until spring 1895, telling of the man-child fully at home in neither the jungle nor the town, amid neither people nor animals, thus reflecting Kipling's own ambivalence.

Mowgli is effectively orphaned twice: by being abandoned and left when his parents flee the tiger; and then being thrown out of the wolf pack. Mowgli encounters a cast of unforgettable creatures: Shere Khan the tiger with his vile sidekick Tabaqui the jackal; Akela the wolf; Baloo the bear; Bagheera the panther; Kaa the python and the Monkey-People who recognise no authority and believe that by chattering about something they have achieved it. Giving unity to this cast of characters is a sense of place, a jungle of central India, and The Law of the Jungle, an ethical code that owes nothing to Christianity – or any of the religions of the East, for that matter.

> Now this is the Law of the Jungle – as old and as true
>   as the sky;
> And the Wolf that shall keep it may prosper, but the
>   Wolf that shall break it must die

As the creeper that girdles the tree-trunks the Law
 runneth forward and back –
For the strength of the Pack is the Wolf and the strength
 of the Wolf is the Pack

… Keep peace with the Lords of the Jungle – the Tiger,
 the Panther, the Bear;
And trouble not Hathi the Silent, and mock not the
 Boar in his lair.

When Pack meets with Pack in the Jungle, and neither
 will go from the trail,
Lie down till the leaders have spoken – it may be fair
 words shall prevail.

When ye fight with a Wolf of the Pack, ye must fight
 him alone and afar,
Lest others take part in the quarrel, and the Pack be
 diminished by war.

The Lair of the Wolf is his refuge, and where he has
 made him his home,
Not even the Head Wolf may enter, not even the Council
 may come …

The Law was not a piece of exotic window-dressing but was integral to the work: Kipling once explained to a literary admirer of The Jungle Book: When I had once found the Law of the Jungle, then all the rest followed as a matter of course.[121]

References to a generalised deity – to God or Allah

– recur through Kipling's work and letters, but he was far less distinct on the central message of Christianity. He had written, to Caroline Taylor when she enquired about his faith, that he believed in a personal God, in the Ten Commandments, but could not believe in eternal punishment or reward. As far as Christianity was concerned he was far from orthodox, being unable to believe in the Trinity or the doctrine of redemption. The nearest he could come to accepting Jesus as Christ was to say he *did voluntarily die in the belief that the human race would be spiritually bettered thereby,* which falls short of the belief required by any but the most extreme liberal sects.[122] He had certainly rejected the narrow evangelicalism of Mrs Holloway, but also the Methodism of his own family.

The Brattleboro townspeople knew he went neither to church nor chapel but felt their distinguished neighbour could not be irreligious so declared that he wrote hymns on a Sunday morning. This was not entirely fanciful, for he wrote his poems to hymn tunes that had formed the standard musical repertory in a Methodist family such as his and in the Calvinist household in Mrs Holloway's house. He certainly felt the need to thank God for his present happiness. At the end of 1893 he wrote in Carrie's diary, *Another perfect year ended. The Lord has been very good to us. Amen.* [123]

Kipling, Carrie and Josephine returned to England in 1894 to visit his parents, now in retirement in Tisbury, Wiltshire. He was already the supreme literary figure, widely feted and invited to join aristocratic and military circles as well as literary ones, a real distinction for a man still only 29. He had been 'sounded' for the position of poet laureate, vacant following the death of Tennyson in 1892, but declared he had no interest in the post, the first of many times he was to refuse a national honour.

The Jungle Book was published in May 1894 when he was in Britain. He delighted that he had confounded the critics who could not understand what kind of a book it was. *The reviews are rather funny,* he wrote, *They don't know how or at which end to pick the thing up.*[124]

He looked with mild curiosity at *The Yellow Book*, first published this year, but was more interested in meeting Aubrey Beardsley with whom he struck up an acquaintance. Kipling's own drawings were significantly similar to Beardsley's; they had developed quite independently but, like Beardsley, had started under Pre-Raphaelite influence.

He made a rare appearance on a public platform as guest of honour at his old school, the United Services College, on the retirement of Cormell Price. While he had a gift for communicating with younger children, he lacked the right touch with teenagers with whom he tried to communicate in inappropriate schoolboy slang. The head prefect who took him around recollected that 'he seemed to be silently looking into the past, and didn't speak for longish periods.'[125] He was, in fact, thinking about a book set in his schooldays.

Back in Brattleboro, as his fame grew, the Kiplings had to contend with sightseers and with ever-resourceful and determined journalists eager to obtain any scrap of information about the reclusive writer. Perhaps surprisingly considering his own early profession of journalism (and Balestier's) and his continuing relationship with publications such as Henley's *National Observer*, Kipling hated journalists. He was churlish about their questions and resented their intrusion into his life, as if he feared the disclosure of real secrets.

He described his method of dealing with a reporter: *It was exactly like talking to a child – a very rude little child. He would begin every sentence with 'Now tell me something about India' and would turn aimlessly from one question to the other without the least continuity. I was very angry, but keenly interested. The man was a revelation to me. To his questions I returned answers mendacious and evasive. After all it really did not matter what I said. He could not understand.*[126] One young woman reporter from a major New York newspaper struggled through snow drifts in a sleigh and called at the door of Naulakha. Thinking her a lost traveller, Carrie Kipling gave her every hospitality until she announced her aim: 'I have come to interview Rudyard Kipling!' Carrie called the butler and said, 'Johnson, see that this lady's conveyance is at the door at once' and wished her good day.[127]

In December 1894 Carrie's accounts show Kipling had made $25,000 that year. A second collection off Mowgli stories was produced in 1895, making Kipling another fortune. Macmillan published 35,000 copies for the day of publication on the strength of advance orders alone. He was not interested in milking success, however, and when he had no further inspiration for writing these stories, he stopped doing so. In November 1895 he wrote, *That ends up Mowgli and there isn't going to be any more to him.*[128] Kipling had no apparent fear of his imagination drying up, he seemed to have an inexhaustible fount of ideas for stories, and was only limited by the time he had to spend writing them.

Kipling's next big project, in 1896, was *Captains Courageous*, his only book in which all the characters and settings are American, something he was able to achieve with the confidence of four years residence in the US. Kipling had encountered a spoiled American child, the son of a millionaire, on his trip from Calcutta to San Francisco with the Hills in 1889. He had kept this character in his mind and developed him into Harvey, a rich youngster who falls overboard from an Atlantic passenger ship, is picked up by a fishing boat and is forced to live and work on the boat until they return to harbour. His character is reformed by the company of the tough but wise sea fishermen and the doctrine of hard work.

Kipling was given local colour and information from Dr James Conland, a neighbour who had delivered Josephine and himself had a close connection to the sea, having been rescued from a shipwreck as a baby. Conland brought Kipling a dead haddock, which he eviscerated in front of the writer in the manner of the cod-fishers off Newfoundland, which became part of the vivid description of gutting cod in the book. Kipling and the doctor went on a field trip to the fishing town of Gloucester, Massachusetts. There he attended the Annual Memorial Service to the men lost in the cod-fishing schooner fleet.

While *Captains Courageous* was presented as a novel, the novel form continued to elude Kipling. It is really a long short story about a boy growing up and learning the lessons of life, albeit in particularly colourful surroundings. As Kipling himself recognised, *There ain't two cents worth of plot in the blessed novel – it's all business.*[129] The book, however, had action, colour and simple character development that made it well suited to screen treatment. A successful film was made with Spencer Tracey in 1937 and it was filmed again in 1996.

Kipling had been thinking of taking out American citizenship and was said to be developing an American accent. He had met President Cleveland, whose standards of public life he deplored, *a colossal agglomeration of reeking bounders* and the future President Theodore Roosevelt, who was much more to his liking as a vigorous man of action.[130] Two towns were named after Kipling in Michigan in 1895, Rudyard and Kipling, marking the high point of his public acclaim in the US. Their second child, Elsie, was born on 2 February 1896.

The family feud
Kipling never got over the notion he developed on his first travels in America that the land was a place of lawless violence. While he did meet some refined, literary Americans, the American he saw most frequently was Beatty Balestier, who was a drunken and often reckless character, but for all his cherished reputation as a wild man, his ever-helpful and generous character endeared him to his farming neighbours.

As the Kiplings became wealthier, Carrie became more English in her habits, dressing for dinner even when only the two of them were present and driving around in her elegant two-horse carriage with a straight-backed English groom in attendance. This was in keeping with the aspirations of the Balestier family in general, with the exception of their boisterous neighbour Beatty, who was the opposite of the conservative, temperate and privacy-loving Kiplings.

While the roots of the problem that split the Balestier family and led to Kipling's departure from America could be put down to simple mutual incompatibility, it is as well to remark that not many people would have wanted Beatty Balestier as a neighbour. As Frederic van de Water, an American journalist wrote, 'Beatty had horses and cattle, a hired man and a hired girl, a daughter, his first wife and a mighty thirst when he welcomed the Kiplings to Vermont. One by one in the years that followed, he lost them all but the last.'[131]

Beatty was well on the way through the first fortune he had inherited when Naulakha was completed. He had been kept by the Kiplings as their agent, superintending the construction and bulk-buying coal and other supplies for the establishment. Carrie directly accused Beatty of appropriating money he had been given for paying Naulakha workmen. As an older sister she tried to keep him on a tight rein, giving him money in small amounts and lecturing him about his wayward lifestyle. It is an example of her unsubtle methods that she tried to persuade Mrs Balestier to join her in removing their names from the backing of Beatty's mortgage, which would have rendered him bankrupt and, so Carrie seemed to believe, would have taught him a lesson. Mrs Balestier refused, remarking with more wisdom than her daughter, 'Beatty is a gentleman, drunk or sober.'[132]

Finally the respectable couple, probably at Carrie's behest, formulated a plan for the reformation of the wastrel, which was taken to Beatty by Kipling. If Beatty would leave his drinking cronies in Vermont and devote himself to work elsewhere, Kipling would support Beatty's wife and child for a year. Beatty was the opposite of grateful. He explained in the most explicit terms what his brother-in-law could do with his charity, and the relationship between them was cool thereafter. As early as May 1895 Carrie records in her diary that the Balestiers 'slammed and locked front door in my face.'

A second cause of conflict was land. Kipling had worried that a small piece of land opposite Naulakha might fall into the hands of someone who would build on it and block his view. Beatty had no intention of selling; he wanted the land for hay for his stock, giving it to Kipling for a dollar if Kipling would allow him to keep mowing it.

Beatty then heard that the Kiplings had had a landscape architect up and were going to turn the mowing land into a formal garden. He invited them to dinner and asked about it, and Carrie said it was true. Beatty told his sister, 'You are in my house; you're my guest but by Christ, once you've left it, I'll never speak to you again as long as I live.'

For the next year Beatty did no more work for the Kiplings and his fortunes fell as Kipling's rose. They were no longer friendly, but by common consent, it was a failure of reticence on Kipling's part that heated enmity into battle. Kipling stopped by for a drink in a hotel, Brooks House, and spoke to a Colonel Goodhue. The conversation turned to Beatty and Kipling said, *Beatty is his own worst enemy. I've been obliged to carry him for the last year; to hold him up by the seat of his breeches.*

The words got back to Beatty and he confronted Kipling on the road to Brattleboro where Kipling was riding his bicycle and he was driving his trap. Kipling heard him out and said, *Let's get this straight. Do you mean personal violence?* Beatty confirmed that he did indeed, unless Kipling retracted the remarks he had made about Beatty he would do something – quite what he threatened was disputed. Kipling said it was to shoot his brains out; Beatty said it was 'the licking of his life.' Kipling would only respond, *You will have only yourself to blame for the consequences.*[133]

Kipling returned to Naulakha to consult Carrie, whose counsel could be relied upon in everything except matters affecting Beatty. The following Saturday while Beatty was out in Brattleboro with his wife and daughter, he was arrested for 'assault with indecent and opprobrious names and epithets and threatening to kill' Kipling. If Kipling hoped the dispute would be thus contained and Beatty would accept a warning, he had poorly misjudged the man. Beatty did not crave the quiet life as did Kipling; he loved being the centre of attention and the bigger the audience for his vindication the better. As Kipling was now one of the most famous writers in the world, and the world had hitherto been starved of personal information about him, the audience for this squabble could be very large indeed.

Beatty was brought to court to face his accuser in front of the Justice of the Peace and Town Clerk William S

Newton. He admitted calling Kipling various names and threatening him with a licking. With a prima facie admission of the offence, the Justice had no alternative but to hold Beatty against a surety, but Beatty was not willing to put up a surety, he asked only for some time to say goodbye to his wife and child before they put him in jail.

A man with far less imagination than Kipling could by now see how this would look: an impecunious native of this town was being torn from the bosom of his family at the instigation of his rich and famous but cruel foreign kinsman. Kipling produced his cheque book and said he would be happy to supply the bail. Beatty refused. He was finally released on his own recognisance. He did not look like a man who was being beaten into seeing the error of his ways.

The case was scheduled to be heard on 12 May 1896, two days hence, giving the local correspondents ample time to file reports and reporters from national newspapers all the time they needed to descend on Brattleboro. Kipling's surly behaviour towards journalists, his failure to endear himself to the townspeople and his generally negative attitude towards American culture told against him. Now the journalists, the townspeople and robust American culture rounded. The town took on the air of a festival, with all the locals coming to enjoy the show, with curious outsiders and the ranks of the press augmenting the crowd. Beatty had met pressmen at the station and driven them to his house to be entertained within sight of Naulakha. The courthouse was overwhelmed and the hearing had to be adjourned to the town hall.

Under relentless questioning from Beatty's counsel Kipling had to admit that he and Beatty had not spoken for a year before the angry encounter; that he had uttered the provocative insults about Beatty; that he had never known Beatty to go about armed; that even at the height of his rage Beatty had not got down from his carriage to make a threat manifest; and that he had given Kipling time to make an apology before the matter proceeded any further.

Kipling was further obliged to admit that for the previous year he had not been supporting his brother-in-law and any loans he had given Beatty had been repaid in full, so even the substance of the remarks he had made, which had enraged Beatty, were not true. He insisted, however, that he felt in danger of his life at Beatty's hands. His defence that all he did was in Beatty's own interest seemed thin and insincere: *I came here for that purpose – to help that boy all I could: if Beatty would stop drinking and go to work. It's what I stayed here for, the reason I settled here in preference to anywhere else in America.*[134]

Kipling refused to acknowledge what now seemed glaringly obvious, what Beatty's counsel urged upon him: if Kipling had only publicly apologised to Beatty, none of this would have happened.

The hearing lasted all day and found there was sufficient in the case to set it before a Grand Jury, which would be held in September. Beatty was bailed for $400 and bound over to keep the peace. This was supposedly a victory for Kipling but he had lost the peace he had previously enjoyed at Naulakha, and he had been held up to public ridicule. It was, as any literate observer could tell, an utterly Kiplingesque tale: the reclusive and somewhat pompous outsider trying to teach his wayward brother-in-law some respect. The brother-in-law calmly let his instructor puff himself up to the full extent of his powers and then slowly deflate in front of an amused crowd.

The day following the trial, 13 May 1896, Carrie's diary showed Kipling literally prostrate with misery: 'Rud a total wreck. Sleeps all the time, dull and listless and dreary. These are dark days for us.'[135] Four days after the trial, however, he was writing, *as to the 'nightmare' it is behind me, and I find myself slowly recovering.*[136]

As Kipling was now to discover, America is not lawless, but suffers from the opposite complaint: stoked by armies of lawyers, litigation never ends. Kipling was now going to have to give court testimony twice: in front of a Grand Jury in September and then publicly again at the trial if the Grand Jury ordained there should be one.

In the following months Kipling did not venture out, even on to his own land, without the protection of a friend. It became obvious that he was mentally unfit to face a public trial. The peace of Naulakha was shattered, the atmosphere irrevocably poisoned and the Kiplings' life overrun with reporters and sightseers. As Kipling wrote, *I prefer to run my own life and do not care for beats on ten dollars a week calling themselves brother-journalists and investigating my back yard and under clothing on the strength of it.*[137]

It is by no means clear how the decision to leave was made; it was probably done jointly. Kipling was writing on 19 August that their passage to England was booked on the first day of September. The family gathered up a small amount of personal possessions and hastened away out of Brattleboro, then Vermont, then the United States. He would never again see the beloved home he had built.

Triumph and Disaster

The family settled for almost a year in Maiden-combe near Torquay, in a rented house they never liked. The cold and the sea air of a provincial town must have brought recollections of Southsea and the House of Desolation. Comparisons with the bliss of Naulakha were inevitable even without little Josephine asking when they were going home. They had made no definite decision not to do so but at the end of 1896 Carrie remarked that not only did Kipling not talk of Brattle-boro, he never even 'reads a letter from America or does anything which remotely reminds him of that last year of calamity and sorrow.'[138]

Kipling treated his misery with doses of nostalgia and humour. He embarked on the *Stalky & Co* stories, partly stimulated by a visit from Cormell Price. His cousin Florence Macdonald was permitted to sit while he was working on the stories and she later furnished a description of him writing relentlessly then laying down his pen and roaring with laughter. He would read a passage to her and she would laugh too. *Come on, Florence,* he would say, *What shall we make them do now?*[139]

The Stalky stories have not worn so well as other Kipling prose work, despite the enduring success of stories based on boarding school life (the Harry Potter tales being an obvious 21st century example). The stories are mainly about the battle of wits between masters and boys in the small world of a boarding school, the wheezes, practical jokes and slang. The three friends, Stalky, M'Turk and Beetle are more recognisably real boys than many fictional children in the way they delight in getting out of work, smoking, drinking and swearing.

The Stalky tales unsubtly show how life at the United Services College was training for frontier warfare. For example in 'Slaves of the Lamp', Stalky and company set two enemies against each other (resulting in a master's study being wrecked) by making each think they have each been attacked by the other. In a later-life counterpart to this story Stalky, a lieutenant on the frontier, is defending a fort which is attacked by two native tribes which he turns against each other by making each think the other is attacking them.

Excursions out of bounds are a rehearsal for reconnoitring enemy terrain; classics are a means to pass the army entrance exam, but also teach the heroic virtues of the imperial Romans. Projecting the imperial theme forward, Kipling takes brief glances forward to see the fate of the boys, for example in 'The Flag of their Country' a character makes a remark, *not forseeing that three years later he should die in the Burmese sunlight outside Minhla Fort.*

The morality of empire is also taught. Three boys, tacitly encouraged by the school's clergyman, use a subterfuge to tie up two other boys and then torture them for being bullies. As H G Wells commented, 'Before resorting to torture, the teaching seems to be, see that you pump up a little justifiable moral indignation, and all will be well. If you have the authorities on your side, then you cannot be to blame. Such, apparently, is the simple doctrine of this typical imperialist.'[140]

Critical opinion was mixed, some finding the book terrific fun, others advising it should be kept out of the hands of impressionable boys. The most extreme view was expressed by critic Robert Buchanan: 'Only the spoiled child of an utterly brutalised public could possibly have written *Stalky & Co* or, having written it, have dared to publish it.'[141]

A volume of verse, *The Seven Seas*, was published in 1896, to public enthusiasm if not critical acclaim. The reaction against Kipling was settling in, that refined critics found his work flashy, vulgar and even brutal, while the public just kept on buying it.

In summer 1897 Rudyard and Carrie moved with Josephine and Elsie to The Elms at Rottingdean in Sussex, the start of an almost 40-year residence in the county. Their third and last child, John Kipling – the only boy – was born there on 17 August 1897. Aunt Georgie and Burne-Jones, now a baronet, and Stanley Baldwin who had married, also lived in Rottingdean, then a quiet fishing village. It was the presence of a literary celebrity, however, that brought curious day trippers who would take away pieces of the ivy that grew on the high wall around The Elms as souvenirs.

The village horse bus went past the wall and overhanging trees hit passengers on the open top deck, so the driver asked the conductor to stop and break off the branches. Another version of this story is that the conductor would deliberately stop the bus and point out The Elms as Kipling's house and encourage passengers to look in to see the great man at work. Whatever the cause, Kipling saw and sent a stiff letter to the bus's owner, which was delivered while he was in the Royal Oak public house. He promptly sold it for 30 shillings and requested that Kipling should send him more letters of complaint. There were so many autograph hunters that Carrie had attempted to limit them by selling Kipling's autograph but it was an ill thought-out scheme, attracting criticism for the Kiplings' apparent greed at a time when he was probably the best paid author in the world.

Recessional

Amid the excitement and pageantry of Queen Victoria's diamond jubilee commemorating 50 years of her reign, Kipling wrote 'Recessional', subtitled '1897'. A recessional is the hymn sung while the clergy and choir withdraw from the chancel. Kipling presents a reflection on empire which warns of the hubris of a nation 'drunk with sight of power.' In a recognition that empires which have risen must fall, he notes:

> Far-called, our navies melt away;
>> On dune and headland sinks the fire:
> Lo, all our pomp of yesterday
>> Is one with Nineveh and Tyre!

Controversial lines referred to *Such boastings as the Gentiles use,/Or lesser breeds without the Law*, which is puzzling. It seems very close to Mowgli's Law of the Jungle: though calling on God (*Judge of the Nations, spare us yet*) makes it clear it is His Law that is referred to.

The ambiguities in the verse are probably best attributable to the speed at which Kipling wrote it. It was said to have been retrieved from Kipling's wastepaper basket by a visitor who was impressed, so Kipling revised it there and then, with suggestions from the others present, and wrote at the bottom of the manuscript: *done in council at North End House, July 16 Aunt Georgie/Sallie/ Carrie and me.*[142] Aunt Georgie (Lady Burne-Jones) took a fresh copy to London and sent it to the *Times* that evening, which printed it the next day. Kipling therefore had little time for the revision of a verse that had previously been consigned to the garbage.

Its effect was startling, immediately making Kipling into a poet of controversy and thoughtfulness. Sir Walter Besant wrote, 'The people, bewildered with pride, were ready to shout they knew not what – to go they knew not whither. And then the poet spoke, and his words rang true. I know of no poem in history so opportune, that so went home to all our hearts – that did its work and delivered its message with so much force.'[143] Kipling refused all payment for it, as he generally did for what he called 'serious' poems; Trix described his 'very strong feelings about his Daemon and the possibility of a gift used unworthily being withdrawn.'[144]

Kipling had been elected to the refined gentlemen's club the Athenaeum in April 1897. He was the youngest member, a recognition of the public importance he had assumed, there was an assumption that he would make public pronouncements of national importance in his work and he had not disappointed. The night of his election he dined with Cecil Rhodes, the South African-based millionaire, and Sir Alfred Milner, recently appointed Queen's High Commissioner in Cape Town. Both had a mission of developing the empire in South Africa and Kipling's assistance was eagerly sought.

The whole family went to South Africa at beginning of 1898 and stayed until April. Kipling was now adding a fourth continent to the three in which he had lived and about which he had written, though Africa would not prove as productive as had been his time in India, London and the United States. Kipling was already developing extreme views about the Boers, of Dutch descent, who controlled the Orange Free State and the Transvaal while the British ran the Cape Colony under Milner. Kipling complained about Johannesburg: *the white man there is slave to the Boer; and the state of things turned me sick. They are without votes: and forbidden to carry arms.*[145]

Kipling fell completely under the spell of Cecil Rhodes. *Rhodes had a habit of jerking out sudden questions as disconcerting as those of a child – or the Roman Emperor he so much resembled. He said to me apropos of nothing in particular: 'What's your dream?' I answered that he was part of it.*[146] Kipling was succumbing to hero worship, always a weakness, though previously often one which had fed his creativity. In the case of Rhodes, Kipling supplied more material for him than he did for Kipling. The writer explained: *My use to him was mainly as a purveyor of words for he was largely inarticulate. After the idea had been presented – and one had to know his code for it – he* would say: 'What am I trying to express? Say it, say it.' So I would say it, and if the phrase suited not, he would work it over, chin a little down, till it satisfied him.[147] Kipling's position as a great man's speech writer suited him emotionally, through Rhodes's voice he could talk tough and the great man would act it out. It was the beginning of a ten-year relationship with South Africa.

On his return, there were family troubles: Uncle Ned, Sir Edward Burne-Jones, died suddenly of a heart attack, in the arms of Kipling's Aunt Georgie. Kipling said, they called it angina-pectoris and it may have been so: but when a man has worked without rest for forty years, the failure may take any shape. It was good, clean over-work – as good a death on the field as ever man could desire.[148] Later in 1898 Trix had a nervous breakdown and was sometimes silent, sometimes talking nonsense incessantly. Alice Kipling refused to allow her daughter to be treated as mentally ill, as Kipling wrote, nothing has been allowed to be done to cure her, though considering the primitive state of psychiatric treatment at the time, it was probably a blessing that the only 'treatment' she received was rest in a nursing home.[149]

Trix had a sad life. She had been too young to remember the blissful infancy in India that her brother clung to when they were boarded in the House of Desolation. She was left at Southsea for more than ten years and though better treated than her brother, she absorbed some of the narrow religiosity of Mrs Holloway.

Her happiest time was after 1844 when she returned to India and lived with her family where her beauty and wit put her at the centre of Simla society. Her imaginative and nervous disposition was not nurtured by an unhappy marriage to an army officer, John Fleming. The couple returned to England in 1898 and Trix was intermittently mentally ill at least from this time, if not earlier.

She was said to have recovered by the end of 1901 and returned to her husband in India until his retirement from the army. Even when sane, she was described as being 'so unworldly that she seemed to move in a land of phantoms.'[150] She had two novels published, *A Pinchbeck Goddess* in 1897 and *The Heart of a Maid* in 1890, and a book of verse written jointly with her mother in 1902. She would have many recoveries and relapses in her mental condition, which did not settle down until late in life. Perhaps stimulated by family difficulties in England, Carrie resolved to see her own family in the US and to introduce her two new children to the Balestiers. Naulakha had been tended by their groom in the family's absence.

Kipling had also maintained a connection with the US through his continuing battle with copyright pirates and his attention to world affairs. Part of his unhappiness when he lived in America resulted from the Cleveland administration's sabre-rattling towards Britain over a border dispute between British Guiana and Venezuela, which disturbed Kipling to a far greater degree than any such quarrel ought to bother a writer. Now the Spanish-American war had drawn Britain and the US closer again as America invaded Cuba to drive out the Spaniards. The war ended with the Philippines being ceded to America. Kipling, not content with the imperial message in the British Empire, wrote to Roosevelt, a hero of the war and soon to be elected governor of New York State: *Now go in and put all the weight of your influence into hanging on permanently to the whole of the Philippines.*[151]

In support of his campaign to have America become an imperial power he wrote 'The White Man's Burden'.

> *Send forth the best ye breed –*
> *Go bind your sons to exile*
>   *To serve your captive's need;*
> *To wait in heavy harness*
>   *On fluttering folk and wild –*
> *Your new-caught sullen peoples,*
>   *Half devil and half child.*

The Americans were called upon to *search your manhood* to fight *the savage wars of peace*, not biding *Sloth and heathen Folly* in order to work for *another's profit* and *another's gain*, making empire building appear a benign process of self-sacrifice.

Kipling still misunderstood America, which had fought a successful revolutionary war against the British Empire and had no wish for one of their own. With his instinctive lack of sympathy for revolution (or even reform), he was not stirred by such history. The verses are hopelessly dated now; the race theory of human progress which Kipling assumed as unquestionably true was so thoroughly discredited by the Nazis that it is difficult to appreciate what sway it once held over, for example, such progressives as H G Wells, whose *Outline of History* describes the whole of human history in racial terms. Kipling cannot be held up to criticism for holding a view of race which was the common currency of the time. The problem of Kipling's imperial attitudes is more serious and goes to the heart of the vision that motivated his writing.

Even at the time it was evident that the biggest burden the white man bore in empire was the weight of his wallet; imperial expansion was a means of producing wealth by exploiting the raw materials of other nations and creating new markets from their populations. There were certainly benefits connected with religion, education, health and the building of infrastructure, but these were by-products of empire, not its objective. Kipling had seen the assistant railway engineer and the hospital doctor battling heat and disease to do the work in the outposts of empire. He had seen the everyday heroism of fallible men trying to do their best in their work and to deal fairly with the natives, and had reported it as if this were the whole picture. Kipling was both literally and metaphorically short-sighted: close up to the builders of empire, he saw their lives in microscopic detail; when he tried to see the wide vistas it was all a blur of colour and action on which he imposed unrefined political views garnered from a minor public school and the conversation of junior officers. Kipling's short stories with their acute attention to detail tell the truth; the poems attempting a grand view of empire are usually just so much bombast.

American tragedy

The Kipling family crossed the Atlantic early in 1899, in poor weather that left the children and their nurse sick, and the girls particularly weak. On arrival in New York they were detained for hours in the customs house and harried by reporters before they got to their chilly hotel. All the children had colds, though Josephine was the worst.

For the first days they had family business to worry about, a major copyright battle to fight as a company was planning an unauthorised collected edition of Kipling's work, reporters to guard off now *White Man's Burden* was receiving comment in the press, and Beatty Balestier had threatened a $50,000 law suit for malicious prosecution against Kipling.

The children were now diagnosed as having not simple colds, but whooping cough. Carrie went down with fever but quickly recovered. Kipling himself fell ill on 20 February, and was quickly diagnosed as having acute lobar pneumonia. The only positive factor in the illness of the Kipling family was that Carrie's sister Josephine had recently married Theo Dunham, a doctor, who immediately set aside all other work and cared continuously for Kipling.

As Kipling's condition was worsening, their daughter Josephine also developed a high temperature and fever. Their doctor feared complications and Carrie decided to get her away from the hotel, to be cared for in the home of their friends the De Forests on Long Island. Carrie called it 'a moment of conscious agony to stand out from the average.'[152] Frank Doubleday, Kipling's friend and publisher, described it to anxious enquirers: 'Mrs Kipling, exhausted by the care of her husband, is unable to be with her.'[153]

Carrie could now devote all her time to Kipling, about whom she wrote, 'His simple life and decent habits, they say, will count in his favour, but his lifelong tendency to fever makes him rather a difficult patient.' Reporters were bothering them so she arranged to give them a daily bulletin on his health. She had the constant care of Dunham; a specialist he called in; and a day and a night nurse with another nurse who was looking after Elsie, who showed signs of following her father and sister into pneumonia.

One of Kipling's lungs began to solidify, then the inflammation spread from the right lung to the left. He was in the delirium of high fever and frequently babbled. Four days into his illness the daily bulletin from his doctors admitted his condition was 'serious' and the following day reported their 'greatest apprehension for the outcome.'[154] As the second lung solidified from the lower to the upper lobes, respiration became increasingly laboured until his breath came in sobs. Only the use of pure oxygen kept him alive.

Downstairs in the lobby 15 or 20 reporters kept vigil, looked after by Frank Doubleday, who gave them bulletins and dealt with the vast correspondence Kipling's illness generated. The illness of this 33-year-old writer was world news; telegrams and letters of sympathy poured in and were filed by Doubleday. In Britain obituaries were set and ready to be printed as soon as the news of his death came. Outside his hotel on Seventh Avenue crowds gathered, some knelt in prayer and prayers were offered up for Kipling in New York churches.

Caroline kept herself strong, did not break down

and took as much rest and food as possible. She wrote on 27 February, after a week of Kipling's illness: 'No material change. We are making a strong fight and may win or lose any hour.'[155] The following day the crisis came and after hours of agonised struggling for breath Kipling stopped speaking and sank into sleep. The doctors could not tell if this was a recovery or a coma, but his temperature fell: he was past the worst. By 4 March he was out of danger.

John and Elsie both recovered quickly from their illness but Josephine was unable to retain food, so what little strength she had dwindled when the fever was most challenging. She then developed something like dysentery that drained her life away. Carrie doubtless regretted sending her away but there was nothing to be done once the child had been moved, and Carrie was able only once to get away from Kipling's bedside to see her daughter, on 5 March. She wrote in her diary, 'I saw Josephine three times today, morning and afternoon and at 10.30 pm for the last time. She was conscious and sent her love to "Daddy and all"'.[156] Her illness followed the same course as Kipling's but she did not survive the crisis. The following morning, at 6.30, the child died.

She was buried at the cemetery in Fresh Pond, Long Island, Carrie returning from the funeral to Kipling's bedside and concealing her mourning dress with a bright shawl. Carrie felt that the knowledge of Josephine's death would be such a devastating blow to Kipling that it would send him back into illness, so she kept it from him while he was trying to pull his life back together. Amid the rush of letters and telegrams congratulating him. His delirium had been a proleptic Kafkaesque dream of being falsely accused of marital infidelity, arrested on a fake charge and tormented by 'lady reporters', struggling to find places where he is supposed to be, a lynch mob coming for him from whom he has to hide, and travelling by submarine to see R L Stevenson (whose death had greatly saddened Kipling). When he had recovered sufficiently, Kipling had a stenographer called for who took down his dictation of this experience, which fills six printed pages.

Carrie put on a brave face as Kipling recovered and presided over a conspiracy in which everyone but Kipling knew that they were not rejoicing but grieving. Frank Doubleday was chosen or elected to tell his friend. 'It was the hardest task I ever undertook,' he said, 'but it had to be done. I took a seat beside him and told the story in as few words as I could. He listened in silence till I had finished, then turned his face to the wall.'[157]

When confronted with the unbearable, as usual, Kipling suppressed the thought and is said to have permitted no further mention of Josephine. This is broadly accurate, though an exaggeration, as he replied to Ted Hill who wrote him a letter of commiseration, their first contact for almost a decade, *Be thankful that you never had a child to lose. I thought I knew something of what grief meant till that came to me.*[158] His general approach to negative events was to refuse to deal with them publicly, but keep going with the work at hand, as a soldier in battle who cannot stop to grieve over dead comrades.

Kipling recuperated at a small hotel in Lakewood. Carrie went to Naulakha to collect a few belongings.

Beatty, whose threat of legal action was only so much bluster, kept his distance. Whatever their plans had been hitherto, the Kiplings now had to sell the house, so redolent of Josephine's spirit. It was eventually sold to their and Wolcott Balestier's friend, Mary Cabot. Kipling was finally well enough to travel back to Sussex in June, but he would never be the same man. 'Much of the beloved Cousin Ruddy of our childhood died with Josephine and I feel that I have never seen him as a real person since that year,' wrote Kipling's cousin Angela Thirkell, while Trix said, 'after his almost fatal illness and Josephine's death – he was a sadder and a harder man.'[159]

He said goodbye to America in his letter to Ted Hill, *My little Maid loved it dearly (she was almost entirely American in her ways of thinking and looking at things) and it was in New York that we lost her ... I don't think I could face the look of the city again without her.*[160] He was never again to visit the United States.

No End of a Lesson

Kipling had been warned by his doctors after his brush with death that he should not winter in England again and he was planning to revisit South Africa despite the approach of war. The discovery of vast gold seams had led to mass immigration into South Africa, which upset the ethnic balance. The Boers, of Dutch descent, wanted to keep political control in their republics and so imposed an ever-increasing residency qualification before white new arrivals had the vote. In effect this meant that the white immigrants, who produced a high proportion of the wealth of the states and paid the same proportion of taxes, had no representation.

The majority black population and the Indians had no political rights either; but though the natives were armed by both sides in the ensuing conflict, it was a 'white man's war' over the question of which European faction should write the South African constitution. The situation escalated with the sending of British troops to the Cape Colony, which neighboured the Boer republics. Paul Kruger, President of the Transvaal, demanded the British should stop sending troops. As the imperial power could not be dictated to, the British declared war on 11 October 1899.

The Boer War, now officially referred to as the South

African War, lasted from 1899 to 1902. It progressed through three phases. In the first, the British suffered severe setbacks, particularly in the 'Black Week' of 10–15 December 1899 when the Boers beat the British in the field and besieged the British-held towns of Ladysmith, Mafeking and Kimberley.

In the second phase, a new army sent under Lords Roberts and Kitchener relieved the besieged towns and occupied the main Boer cities of Bloemfontein, Johannesburg and Pretoria. The war was declared won.

Finally, Kitchener was left to 'mop up' remaining resistance. For the next 15 months a fierce Boer guerrilla campaign was opposed by a policy of denying the Boers any support in the field and dividing up the country with barbed wire and blockhouses, sweeping the countryside to track down guerrillas. The Boers were finally starved into surrender in May 1902.

The war was opposed by anti-imperialists, who felt it was a militarily pointless conflict being fought for the financial gain of men like Rhodes; and by idealists such as Kipling's Aunt Georgie, who felt it was a brutal attack on a small nation which disgraced the British Empire. It was also opposed by imperialists such as the journalist and campaigner W T Stead, who felt that the Boers had founded outposts of civilisation in Africa and other whites should support them in a civilising mission. Nothing of these reservations permeate Kipling's letters or writing at this time. Fired by the imperial vision of Rhodes, he was a true enthusiast for war, unable to see the least merit in the Boers and feeling that the war would do no end of good in beefing up the British army,

The war is having a splendid effect on the land and all fires will burn more clearly for the fierce draft that has been blown through them, he wrote.[161]

As his contribution to the war effort he wrote 'The Absent-Minded Beggar', a crude and thumping verse, more a song than a poem, and it was duly set to music by Sir Arthur Sullivan in a tune as Kipling said guaranteed to pull teeth out of barrel-organs.[162]

It was a call that patriotism should not be enough, and that soldiers (and their women and children) should be supported by those who cheered them off to war,

> When you've shouted 'Rule Britannia', when you've
>   sung 'God Save the Queen',
> When you've finished killing Kruger with your mouth
> Will you kindly drop a shilling in my little tambourine
> For a gentleman in khaki ordered South?

It was published in the Daily Mail the month war was declared and was, Kipling said, the first time I ever set out of malice aforethought to sell my name for every blessed cent it would fetch.[163] Handkerchiefs, tobacco jars, plates and other items were produced bearing the poem or part of it and sold to raise a quarter of a million pounds for a fund for soldiers and their families. Kipling and Carrie went to the Cape to give tobacco and other comforts to the troops in January 1900 at the height of Boer successes against the British, when even his friend Rhodes was besieged in the town of Kimberley.

Kipling writes with a rare boastful tone of his work in the Boer War, my position among the rank and file came to be unofficially above that of most Generals ... My note-of-hand at the Cape Town depot was good for as much as I cared to take about with me. The rest followed. My telegrams were given priority by sweating R.E. sergeants from all sorts of congested depots. My seat in the train was kept for me by British Bayonets in their shirt-sleeves. My small baggage was fought for and servilely carried by Colonial details, who are not normally meek, and I was persona gratissima at certain Wynberg Hospitals where the nurses found I was good for pyjamas. [164]

Lord Roberts, now in command of the British force in South Africa, had of course known Kipling since his days in India and he knew Kipling's skills could be put to better use than merely distributing tobacco. He sent for Kipling who spent the evening with him and once the Orange Free State capital Bloemfontein had been taken, Kipling was ordered there to meet men from the Times and from Reuters and to edit a paper for the troops. They took over the Boer newspaper, renamed it The Friend, and ordered the reluctant compositors and other staff to get working on Lord Roberts's Official Proclamation to the enemy. Kipling had the satisfaction of picking up from the floor the proof of an article which the Boers had had no time to print, a really rude leader about myself.[165]

Kipling was appalled at the mismanagement of the war, in particular the disease cultivated by incompetence: an exhausted horse battery assigned the site of an evacuated typhoid hospital; drinking water taken from the contaminated Modder River and the organisation of latrines left to the manual workers who dug them. During the poorly executed battle of Paardeberg, Kipling went up with an ambulance train to the railhead at Modder River when the wounded were being evacuated, his first experience of war. He also came under fire for the first time in his life while taking refuge in a farmhouse during an ineffectual engagement by the British attempting to encircle a Boer detachment.

By June 1900 Lord Roberts had taken both the Boer capitals but the Boers fought on. The solution, initiated under Roberts but brought to its zenith under Kitchener who succeeded him, was a scorched-earth policy to destroy the farms, crops and livestock of the Boers so they could no longer live on the land. The Boer women and children were taken to concentration camps, which were widely criticised within Britain and subject to withering attack abroad.

The blackest indictment of Kipling's tendency to shut out pain from his mind and refuse to contemplate Josephine's death was his lack of sympathy with the Boers, whose children were the principal victims of the British concentration camp policy. Some 28,000 people died in the concentration camps, most of them children. Kipling wrote that the Boers were *having the time of their lives – stealing from friends and foes alike and living on the fat of the land ... We are looking after their wives and kids so they have nothing to worry about.*[166] The Boers were in fact maintaining a courageous and resourceful guerrilla war which became a classic of its kind, holding down the imperial force of half a million soldiers with a few thousand men in the field.

His South African experiences did not deliver rich prose for Kipling: he was not given to a detailed understanding of the lives of settlers and their interaction with natives as he had been in India. For the first time on a large scale he had allowed his political views to get in the way of his artistic understanding. At the end of the war Kipling considered the British had done the Boers a good turn, *We put them in a position to uphold and expand their primitive lust for racial domination*, he wrote.[167] How he could reconcile believing this, while simultaneously respecting Rhodes with his racially-based imperialism is beyond reason. In general Kipling felt *the experience has been wholesome. We were bung-full of beastly unjustified spiritual pride as we were with material luxury and over much ease.*[168]

Rhodes had been besieged in Kimberley until February 1900 when Kipling had arrived at the start of the war. When the siege was lifted, he discussed with Kipling his proposed establishment of a house for the use of artists and writers. Carrie went with his architect to choose the site for The Woolsack, on Rhodes's Groote Schuur estate at the Cape. He offered it to the Kiplings for as long as they wanted it and they were to visit each year until 1908, spending English winters walking amid the pine and eucalyptus and watching the animals. The children were particularly delighted with the zebras, a spitting lama and a lion cub, rejected by his mother and henceforth fed by bottle by Carrie, using stout motor-gloves.

Sir George Younghusband recalled meeting Kipling at camp in South Africa, peering through the upper half of his spectacles for distance viewing, walking fast to keep up with Rhodes who was considerably larger. As they were leaving camp the men of the 3rd Imperial Yeo-manry gathered and raised a cheer.

'Take off your cap, they are cheering you' said Rhodes.

No they are not. They are cheering you. Take off your cap, said Kipling.

Someone wisely advised that the men were cheering them both, 'Whereupon both, clinging close together for support, shyly took off their caps.'[169]

Cecil Rhodes was born in England in 1853 and was sent to Africa for his health, which was always delicate. Rejecting a farming life, he moved to Kimberley, the cen-tre of diamond mining, where eventually hard work made him wealthy. He returned to England in 1873 to take an Oxford degree. While there he made his first will, for the founding of a secret society for 'the exten-sion of British rule throughout the world.'

Rhodes founded the De Beers mining company. Though a process of buying out rivals, he came to own 90 per cent of the world's diamond production, and extensive gold interests. He dreamed of building a rail-way from the Cape to Cairo and moved into politics to facilitate further advances. By a series of tricks, dubious treaties and military threat, Rhodes's British South Africa Company eventually dominated the lands of the Shona and the Matabele, which were given his name as Rhodesia.

He became prime minister of the Cape Colony from 1890 to 1896 when his connection with the Jameson raid, intended to stir a rebellion in the Transvaal, forced his resignation. The Boer War led to a questioning of

Rhodes's style of imperialism and his last years were marred by his coming under the spell of a seductive con-woman, Princess Radziwill.

Kipling spent a great deal of time with Rhodes, whose poor health meant he often lay on a couch. He received visitors thus, who would often be waiting for days to be seen, though Rhodes always had time for Kipling, who helped him with the details of the 'Rhodes Scholars' scheme to have men of high character from different parts of the British Empire and the US educated at Oxford. The scholarships have, ironically considering Rhodes's racially superior views, enabled many non-white students to enjoy higher education. Their friendship was short-lived, as Rhodes's health was failing fast. Kipling visited him almost every day during the winter of 1901–2, as he lay dying. Rhodes's heart finally gave up on 26 March 1902, when the empire builder was 49 and the war was not yet won. Kipling wrote: *No words could give you any idea of that great spirit's power or the extent to which the country worshipped him.*[170] Kipling certainly worshipped him – almost literally, for he capitalised the pronoun in a manner normally reserved for deity: *I don't think that anyone who did not actually come across Him with some intimacy of detail can ever realise what He was. It was His Presence that had the Power.*[171]

When the war ended with a day of public celebration in June 1902, on the other side of Rottingdean Square from Kipling Aunt Georgie hung a black banner saying: 'We have killed and also taken possession,' expressing her feelings on the brutal conduct of the war. A crowd of what passed for patriots gathered, trying to pull down the banner and set fire to Lady Burne-Jones's hedge. The disturbance brought Kipling, recently returned from South Africa, rushing across the green to make a speech to calm the demonstrators, who left without further disturbance. It was not the only time after the brush with death in 1899 that he had to display a courage not apparent in him before. A deranged character who believed his mission was to kill Kipling followed him to South Africa and broke into The Woolsack with a revolver late one night. Kipling enticed him to sit down and have a drink before carrying out his duty, and talked with him, giving him whisky until the man fell asleep.

South Africa provided Kipling with inspiration for some of his most memorable verse. The experience of those involved in the war was reflected in 'Dirge of Dead Sisters', commemorating the nurses who died; and 'Boots', an evocation of the march of weary soldiers.

While Kipling was never able to accept that Britain had done anything wrong in the war, his tone after it was more thoughtful. He looked to what had been learned from it:

> Let us admit it fairly, as a business people should,
> > We have had no end of a lesson: it will do us no
> > > end of good.

In 'The Settler', a much finer poem, a British soldier turned farmer reflects as he turns the soil over which he has fought:

> Here where my fresh-turned furrows run,

And where the deep soil glistens red,
I will repair the wrong that was done
To the living and the dead.

His South African connection led him to write lines adulating Milner and Rhodes and his most famous poem, 'If', was inspired by Leander Starr Jameson, whose reckless 'raid' on the Boers almost caused a war four years earlier than the Boer War and was the cause of Rhodes's resignation as the Premier of Cape Colony. Jameson became Prime Minister in 1904 with his official residence on the Groote Schuur estate, which had been bequeathed to the nation by Rhodes. They were therefore neighbours when Kipling was in South Africa, but he was not again to visit the Cape after Jameson lost his position as prime minister to a Boer in 1908. Jameson visited Kipling in Sussex in 1909 and it was after his departure that Kipling, wrote the poem 'If', with some of his most-quoted lines:

If you can keep your head when all about you
Are losing theirs and blaming it on you …

… If you can meet with Triumph and Disaster
And treat those two impostors just the same …

… If you can fill the unforgiving minute
With sixty seconds' worth of distance run …

Its almost biblical intonation and complex rhyme scheme make it Kipling's best-loved poem, still widely quoted and it would be more widely quoted still had not Kipling so clearly masculinised it with the last line – *you'll be a Man, my Son!* though the qualities represented in the poem were embodied perfectly well by Carrie Kipling and other women of Kipling's acquaintance. Kipling was insisting on a gender separation when the western world was moving towards an appreciation of the similarities between men and women, not the differences.

It was doubtless because of his generous actions on behalf of the troops in particular that prime minister Lord Salisbury sent his secretary down to see Kipling in Sussex in 1899 to offer him a knighthood. He refused, as he was to refuse two further times – in 1903 and 1917 – followed by a refusal of the Order of Merit in 1921 and again in 1924.

He also refused to join the royal party when the Prince of Wales went to India in 1903 and again when he went as King in 1911. Why he refused awards from the empire he adored and the monarch he respected is not entirely clear. The official reason was that it might compromise his integrity and restrict his freedom of independent judgement. Kipling's views were extremely well known, however, and no one offering an award was doing so in the expectation that he might become less of a Tory or of an imperialist. The deeper reason is probably Kipling's superstition that his gift was supernatural and he should not tarnish it with such baubles of the world as a KCMG.

He seemed always to accept honorary degrees, however. McGill University in Canada was the first to confer an honorary degree on Kipling, in 1899, and hencefor-ward he took them from the universities of Durham, Oxford, Cambridge, Edinburgh, Strasburg and Athens. He always felt he had missed something by not having a university education and this was some compensation – a recognition from the universities that he really deserved academic distinction and his lack of an undergraduate career was a mere oversight.

As he tried to learn the lessons of the new century, politics took more of his time, which was unhelpful for a creative writer. Politically Kipling was contemptuous of democracy, authoritarian in his conception of good government, in awe of military virtues and scornful of the blessings of peace.

On the practical side he founded the Rottingdean rifle range, largely at his own expense, in order to lead England in 'preparedness' for war by training the local youths to shoot. In the same cause he urged compulsory military drill and mocked England's passion for games when, he felt, the effort could be better engaged in mili-tary training. As he berated the public in 'The Islanders':

> Then ye returned to your trinkets; then ye contented
>   your souls
> With the flannelled fools at the wicket or the muddied
>   oafs at the goals.

Kipling, of course, had been saved from compulsory games at school by his poor eyesight. At least no one could accuse Kipling of courting an easy popularity by saying what people wanted to hear. The editor of Kipling's letters, Thomas Pinney, remarked that 'the hortatory, scolding, even Cassandra-like tone in much of this work began to grate on some of Kipling's public; it is at this time that Kipling starts to wear out the almost overwhelming welcome that he had until then received.'[172] While Kipling was thus parading his prejudices, it is the more remarkable that he was also – during the Boer War – writing his most sophisticated long work in which there is no sign of the blustering conservative of his public life.

The little friend of all the world

The background of Kim had been with Kipling since his days in India and the unsuccessful *Mother Maturin* of 1885, but the notion of the Irish boy born in India and mixed up in native life was created while he was living in America, three times begun and left incomplete. At Rottingdean, and more particularly in Wiltshire when he talked it over with his father, Kipling developed the story of the boy taking a journey through northern India. Kipling said the best of the book, which he clearly loved, was contributed by his father.

Kipling declared that he would use a picaresque form: what was good enough for Cervantes was good enough for him. His mother scorned him, 'Don't you stand in your wool-boots hiding behind Cervantes with *me*! You *know* you couldn't make a plot to save your soul.'[173] This was true; Kipling was a master at the creation of characters and situations which are ideal for short stories, but he had no skill at the game of consequences which is plot making, and plots are considered essential in the modern novel.

Kim was completed in the summer of 1900. It is the last and largest of his works based on an India he had left more than ten years before. It is the story of Kimball O'Hara, the orphaned son of an Irish soldier, and a nursemaid of indeterminate race who finds his home in the bazaar of Lahore: he is *friend of all the world* because he can move with facility across race, caste, religious and class boundaries. He is first encountered sitting astride the antique bronze gun in front of the Lahore Museum (where Lockwood Kipling was curator). He meets a Tibetan lama who seeks a holy river. Kim seeks a red bull in a green field (the symbol of the Mavericks, his father's regiment, though he does not know it) and the two set off on a journey. They go by railway and along the Grand Trunk Road, *such a river of life*, in search of their destiny. Part of the story involves a coded map of the battle formations for an attack on British forces on the north-west frontier, which Kim has been entrusted to carry by a horse dealer who is a spy for the British.

When he finds his father's regiment, Kim is taken in by the army chaplains and sent to school. While the military authorities are eager for Kim to see himself as a sahib, he himself, and his spymaster, see more value in a shape-shifting, multilingual identity. He also has the choice between the Way of the lama's spirituality, and the Great Game of British agents, a choice between contemplation and action, between East and West. Kim is, then, like Mowgli making his choice of the jungle or the village, between two worlds, and one is tempted to see these sympathetic boy characters as manifestations of Kipling's own character.

The sympathy of the book was not only for the lama and Kim, the holy fool and his cunning sidekick. The Indian characters are all drawn with a sensitivity and depth that escapes the depiction of some of the English ones. In particular, Huree Chunder the Babu is an educated Indian of the type Kipling despised, a man always quoting Shakespeare and misusing erudite words. Yet he acquits himself with honour, willingly going into danger as a duplicitous guide for the Russian spies for the sake of the Great Game. He is a character both comic and heroic.

Kim was serialised in *Cassell's Magazine* in Britain and *McClure's Magazine* in the US, then published in book form in both countries. Joseph M Rogers, who worked on *McClure's*, said that Kipling was paid the largest sum ever given an author for serial rights to it. He remembered Kipling still rewriting as the parts came out, 'I know of no author who has a greater tendency to change and change again until it suits him. My recollection is that *Kim* was rewritten five times, three times after it was set in type. I think the most interesting manuscript I ever saw was that of the page-proofs of this book after it had been twice in type. It was filled with marginal corrections, some of minor and some of major importance. The author sought ever to get exactly the right word or phrase for his purpose and that manuscript was a terror to compositors – all the more so because Kipling is extraordinarily particular about having every word and punctuation mark inserted just as he wrote it.'[174]

The reception was muted by controversy over the war and by Kipling's uncertain market: the intellectuals who reviewed books were the sort of people who disdained Kipling's jingoism, even if they were not anti-war. As for Kipling's stalwart supporters, the book's allusive style and sensitive representation of India disconcerted those who were used to Kipling serving them rations of bully beef. On serial publication many readers were simply confused; they wanted more story and less colour.

The book showed to discerning critics, however, that there was more to Kipling than the drum-banging patriot that he was always presenting as his true self. Henry James, who only four years previously had been complaining of Kipling's descent into simpler and simpler subjects, wrote to him, 'I overflow, I beg you to believe, with *Kim*, and I rejoice in such a saturation, such a splendid dose of you ... What a luxury to *possess* a big subject as you possess India ... The way you make the general picture live and sound and shine, all by a myriad touches that are like the thing itself pricking through with a little snap – that makes me want to say to you: "Come, all else is folly – sell all you have and give to the poor!" by which I mean chuck public affairs, which are an ignoble scene, and stick to your canvas and your paint-box. There are as good colours in the tubes as ever were laid on, and *there* is the only truth. The rest is base humbug.'[175]

Kipling himself recognised the book was *a bit more temperate and wise than much of my stuff*, a remark which begs the question that if he knew much of his material was intemperate and unwise, why did he release it?[176]

His own explanation, given in verses 'The Two-Sided Man' used as an epigraph to a chapter is:

Much I owe to the Lands that grew –
More to the Lives that fed –
But most to Allah Who gave me two
Separate sides to my head.

I would go without shirt or shoe
Friend, tobacco or bread
Sooner than lose for a minute the two
Separate sides of my head! [177]

Kipling is saying he recognises his debt to the countries that nourished his imagination – England, India, America, South Africa – and to the people who guided him. Yet the defining characteristic of a dual personality was put in him not by these, but by God. It is more important than comfort and friendship and he will hold on to it. He was still divided between the sensitive poet of the United Services College study and the aspiring soldiers of *Stalky & Co*.

It is easy to condescend to Kipling and tell him in retrospect, as his sophisticated contemporaries did, that he should cultivate the sensitive artist and dismiss the rhyming patriot. Kipling's barely coded response is quite straightforward: both sides of his character are necessary for his life. Whatever his critics say, his duality is not a curse to be rid of, but a God-given boon.

Ghosts Walk

Kipling's productive life in the early 20th century was dominated by home, children and such home-based activities as motoring around Sussex, though the illness and death of family members was to play an increasing part.

Carrie, 39 in 1901, was complaining in her diaries that she was committed to 'grind' while others of the family went out, and she did not enjoy the incessant entertaining as Kipling did, and certainly felt the pressure of having to be agreeable to the in-laws. She had undergone the tremendous effort of caring for Kipling in his near-fatal illness; and the death of their daughter two years previously weighed on her. She must have wondered if things would have gone differently for Josephine if she had kept her close by rather than assuming she had a childhood illness that would pass. Josephine was a dainty child who was fussy about her food, who in her father's eyes could do no wrong, and was perhaps sometimes resented by her mother. It is a reasonable assumption that Carrie felt an immense burden of guilt at the death of her daughter, which must have seemed like a human sacrifice for the life of her husband, a tragedy worthy of Euripides.

Regardless of the exact cause, the fact is that Carrie suffered the torments of the damned, a mental state that intensified when Kipling was away. Kipling knew this and when, for example he was in Tisbury, Wiltshire, seeing his parents, he would write to Carrie sometimes twice a day and telegram as many as four times. Her diary reads: 'July 17 I sink down leagues in my declining stride to reach my actual physical state when not braced by necessity. An awful ghost to live with. 18 Down and down I go.'

Kipling then joined a ship to which he had been invited to observe naval manoeuvres. Carrie continued: 'July 21 Still more down in body my mind doing a series of acts in a circus beyond words to depict in its horrors … 26 I remain empty at the bottom of my collapse I think. 27 I remain stationary at the bottom depth physically … Aug 3 Rud goes to Tisbury [rather than returning to her after the naval exercises]. I cannot realise it – it has shocked me so. August 4 Dreadful night trying not to think out the black future. August 5 Rud means to stop longer away. August 6 A night of mental agony leaves me down in the bottom of the pit and well nigh hopeless for the black future.'[178] Carrie's instability was to increase as time passed, unsettling her relationship with Kipling.

'There is no doubt that her difficult temperament sometimes reacted adversely on my father and exhausted him,' wrote Elsie, 'but his kindly nature, patience and utter loyalty to her prevented his ever questioning this bondage, and they were seldom apart.'[179]

Jerome K Jerome recalled a holiday in Engelberg, Switzerland with the Kiplings. Jerome had known Carrie Kipling before her marriage and felt that now 'She was still a beautiful woman, but her hair was white. There had always been sadness in her eyes, even when a girl.'[180] This is not to say that gloom had utterly descended on the family. Jerome described how during poor weather he devised private theatricals in which little John played a suffragette, Elsie a costermonger's girlfriend with Kipling acting as scene shifter.

Doubtless like other parents who have lost children, the Kiplings kept their misery to themselves in order to make the best of life for the two who remained. Josephine's death made an already present interest in the afterlife more poignant, though Kipling's fascination for the subject long preceded the death of loved ones – the ghost story 'The Phantom Rickshaw' of 1885 was one of his first published pieces. Another view of the afterlife, that of endless oriental-style reincarnation was offered in 'The Finest Story in the World' in 1891. In 'Wireless' of 1903 a consumptive and lovesick apothecary goes into an opium dream and recites verses from 'The Eve of St Agnes', which he has never read. While this is taking place, early experiments in radio are being conducted in a back room but the operators find the message they receive is Keats's poem. The apothecary is experiencing what would be called the 'channelling' of the souls of dead individuals; the radio operator is dealing with EVP, electronic voice phenomenon, a belief that modern technology allows communication with the dead. Kipling was, as usual, up to date with his technical know-how – radio communication with the dead was a matter of discussion at the time, even Thomas Edison is said to have believed in it.

Kipling saw his lost child everywhere in his Rotting-dean house; he told his mother how 'he saw her when a door opened, when a space was vacant at table, coming out of every green dark corner of the garden'.[181] It was this eerie, comforting yet shocking relationship with the dead that stimulated one of his finest stories, 'They' of 1904, which brings together Kipling's interests in motoring and exploring the English countryside and merges them with the brooding contemplation of lost children.

The story is merely that a motorist loses his way and calls at a manor house where he observes children watching. The blind owner of the house teasingly remarks that she can only hear them. Given copious clues, on further visit he realises the children are dead. With particular poignancy, the only child who touches him is a little girl: *I felt my relaxed hand taken and turned softly between the soft hands of a child … The little brushing kiss fell in the centre of my palm – a gift on which the fingers were, once, expected to close: as the all-faithful half-reproachful signal of a waiting child not used to neglect even when the grown-ups were busiest.* This was drawn from life. As Ted Hill described 'this was the little cere-mony that his beloved dead daughter had observed whenever she wanted to be near him, yet saw that he was too busy to be disturbed.'[182]

The Kiplings had become unhappy at The Elms. It was too reminiscent of the dead: of both Josephine and their neighbour Ned Burne-Jones, and Kipling's fame brought an incessant stream of curious trippers to see Kipling and his family as if they were living exhibits. Kipling and Carrie motored around the country of

Sussex, heavily veiled against the dust on the unmade roads, looking for a new place to live. The house they liked most was Bateman's, a Jacobean stone house on a small estate just south of Burwash. They wanted it as soon as they saw it, but it had just been let for a year and so they had to wait, and eventually purchased it for £9,300 in June 1902.

There was the date AD 1634 over the door of the beamed, panelled house with an oak staircase and huge arched fires. At the bottom of the walled garden was a weed-choked river. As there was no electricity and Kipling was eager to have all modern conveniences, they had to try to install a generator themselves. Kipling hoped to do so using the power of the stream through the mill that stood on their land. With his usual tendency to call on great men to help him, Kipling asked Sir William Willcocks who designed the Aswan Dam (now the Aswan High Dam) if they could run a turbine with the power from the stream. The civil engineer advised they could if they cleared the stream and dug a trench to take the cable. The system ran for 25 years, after which it was slightly worn so they replaced it, but they never again had anything so reliable.

Kipling was delighted at ordering work on the house from the Sussex natives, who he regarded with as much amused detachment as he had the Indian natives. He thought England wonderful and delighted in the fact that at last he was one of the gentry. Kipling had first hired a car in December 1899 and began his tours of Sussex, in the early days sometimes at the dizzy speed of eight miles an hour, in vehicles which spat water and boiling oil. He bought his first car, a Locomobile, in 1901 and afterwards always had a vehicle, finally settling for a Rolls Royce. He never drove himself, always using a chauffeur (who was also skilled as a mechanic), which was something of a necessity in those early days when there was a breakdown on most trips. Kipling persevered despite the problems, with what many felt was a short-term gimmick, describing his *agonies, shames, delays, rages, chills, parboilings, road-walkings, water-drawings, burns and starvations*.[183] He knew enough of engineering to realise that he must persevere; motor cars would improve progressively. There was often a certain hilarity on the part of his friends, to whom he had extolled the virtues of the car, however. He visited Henry James in nearby Rye and promised to call to take him to lunch at Bateman's then take him back home in time for tea. Inevitably, given such boasting, the car seized up there and then and Kipling had to wire to Birmingham for a mechanic who came to Rye to fix the vehicle. The Kiplings went home by train.

He was clearly not one of those conservatives who repudiated technology. His discovery of England in the early 20th century, as reflected in his stories as well as his life, was the exploration of a nation in an advanced stage of industrial revolution, just set to be changed utterly by easily available electricity, the internal combustion engine and the new media of cinema and wireless, all of which he wove into stories.

In his early years at Bateman's he wrote 'Mrs Bathurst', in which a naval officer obsessively revisits the cinema to see a short flash of a woman he once loved.

Kipling then turned his mind to what would soon be called Science Fiction. In 1905 he wrote 'With the Night Mail' about an airship crossing the Atlantic and wrote a development of the story, 'As Easy As A.B.C.' in 1907. This is a vision of 2065 (200 years after Kipling's birth) in which the Aerial Board of Control, an international company of technicians, has taken over the earth. Moral obsessions are with the prevention of crowds and the protection of privacy; shame and reticence are the highest virtues. The Board, based in London, is called to send a fleet of flying war machines to Chicago to deal with an outbreak of democracy: people assembling in crowds, making speeches and casting votes. The fleet asserts control by incinerating part of the city: *It was as though the floor of Heaven had been riddled and all the inconceivable blaze of suns in the making was poured through the manholes.* The few fledgling democrats who are left, huddled together and still making speeches of defiance, are taken away as prisoners. In a brilliant satirical twist, one of their captors decides to use them as a live show for the entertainment of the public – making speeches and organising votes in what would be broadcast as a comedy routine.

The work is startlingly original, and as a vision of a totalitarian state looks forward to Yevgeny Zamyatin's *We* of 1924 and Huxley's *Brave New World* of 1932. The only contemporary comparison was with H G Wells, who had a surprisingly similar career trajectory to Kipling, including becoming obsessed with using his literary gifts to deliver a political message. Kipling had read Wells's *Anticipations of the Reaction of Mechanical and Scientific*

Progress Upon Human Life and Thought of 1901 with its government of authoritarian technocrats, and sent him a cordial letter about it.

Just so

The first years of the 20th century saw Kipling's further development as a writer for children. Kipling had always told stories to his children, since Josephine was small, refining them with re-telling.

The Just So Stories developed from stories he told small audiences of children on passages towards the Cape on the family's annual journeys to South Africa. They were fantastic tales about the evolution of things in which animals and inanimate objects interact with one another and with humans. The complex and absurd word play enchanted children, while mocking Darwinian evolutionary theory entertained adults.

'How the Whale got his Throat', for example, starts: In the sea, once upon a time, O my Best Beloved, there was a Whale, and he ate fishes. He ate the starfish and the garfish, and the crab and the dab, and the plaice and the dace, and the skate and his mate, and the mackerel and the pickereel, and the really truly twirly-whirly eel. All the fishes he could find in all the sea he ate with his mouth – so! Till at last there was only one small fish left in all the sea, and he was the small 'Stute Fish, and he swam a little behind the Whale's right ear, so as to be out of harm's way.

The stories are full of fragments of Eastern mythology, of magicians, afrits and djinns; and of people defined by their religion or nationality: the Parsee and the rhinoceros; the Ethiopian and the leopard; The Most Wise

Sovereign Suleiman-bin-Daoud. Kipling was so fond of these stories that he illustrated them himself, the only book for which he did so. Immediately on publication, in 1902, Kipling recovered the critical praise that he had lost by 'indifferent verse' and the Stalky stories. The paradox of such vastly different material emerging from the same pen was described by G K Chesterton, 'Mr Rudyard Kipling is a most extraordinary and bewildering genius … just as we are in the afterglow of a certain indignation against this stale, bitter modernity which had begun to appear in Mr Kipling's work, we come upon this superb thing, the *Just So Stories* … he has written new legends.'[184]

More new legends inspired by his discovery of the English countryside came in the form of *Puck of Pook's Hill* in 1905. The idea for a specifically history-based series of tales came from Kipling's cousin, Ambrose Poynter, who urged Kipling to 'Write a yarn about Roman times here … about an old Centurion of the Occupation telling his experiences to his children.'[185] Kipling liked the idea and struggled to make something of a fictionalised eye-witness history but discarded three stories using this technique until he tried to put it behind him and *the whole thing linked itself*. The result was *Puck of Pook's Hill*, named after a hill they could see from their house, more properly known as Perch Hill. The character for Puck came from a playlet Kipling organised for his children involving characters from Shakespeare's *Midsummer Night's Dream*. In the story cycle Una and Dan (Elsie and John) conjure up Puck by performing the play three times in a fairy ring on Midsummer Night's

Eve. He tells tales of the Romans, the Norman Conquest and the heathen god Weland in a magical history in which fairies and deities co-exist with fictional characters who Kipling sets in the real landscape of Sussex and against real or conjectured events.

Kipling viewed his motor car as a time machine empowering the landscape to come to life like a living museum. He wrote, *I can go from the land of the Ingoldsby Legends by way of the Norman Conquest and the Barons' War into Richard Jefferies' country, and so through the Regency … On a morning I have seen the Assizes, javeline-man and all, come into a cathedral town; by noon I was skirting a new-built convent for expelled French nuns; before sundown I was watching the Channel Fleet off Selsea Bill, and after dark I nearly broke a fox's back on a Roman road … in England the dead, twelve coffin deep, clutch hold of my wheels at every turn, till I sometimes wonder that the very road does not bleed.*[186]

Just So Stories had been told to the children when they were small; as Elsie and John grew older the stories became more sophisticated. *Puck of Pook's Hill* was published when they were nine and ten, *Rewards and Fairies* when they were 13 and 14. These last stories Kipling described as having *to be read by children, before people realised that they were meant for grown-ups*, a devious aim which is doubtless the reason for the stories' lack of success compared to his earlier work for children.[187] He explained to a correspondent that the central idea was expressed by every chief character in the stories as 'What else could I have done? … My notion was to give an idea of the way in which the land itself compels the men it breeds to* serve it in some fashion or another.[188] Kipling communicated best with the very young. He was an early supporter of his friend Robert Baden-Powell's Boy Scout Movement, for whom he wrote the 'Patrol Song' in 1909, but the best memorial to Kipling in the lives of the young is the use of names from the Jungle Book in the organisation of the Boy Scouts' junior offshoot, the Cubs.

He liked to recite verse for his children, to such an extent that quotations from Longfellow and Wordsworth became part of their everyday talk. Elsie remembered how in South Africa she used to read Kipling to sleep for his afternoon siesta, paying particular attention to the pronunciation of words as he always insisted, until he was too sleepy to bother about it, 'but when a specially long or difficult word had to be dealt with, the ruthless, wide-awake child would rouse her father to ask how it should be pronounced.'[189] There is no indication in the accounts of Elsie and John's childhood that either of the children were as bright or so clearly destined for literature as was the lost Josephine.

Kipling later contributed to Oxford historian C R L Fletcher's A School History of England, a beautifully illustrated example of what would later be disdained as the Whig interpretation of history. Kipling wrote poems to accompany text in which Fletcher occasionally expressed racial views that were intemperate even compared to Kipling's. The poet may well have written the last chapter, which describes the coming of the machines in the Industrial Age.

Hammer of the Liberals

In terms of public life, Kipling's fortunes were at a low ebb in the early years of the 20th century. His volume *The Five Nations* was published in 1903, containing some of his most strident imperial verse: 'The White Man's Burden' and 'The Islanders', as well as the more contemplative 'Recessional' and 'The Settler'. Its title was parodied as Kipling's Five Notions 'and every one of 'em is wrong.'[190]

Kipling was the trumpeter of nation, empire and the 'white race', a role which a diminishing number now found attractive. While patriotism was still a strong collective emotion after the Boer War, the imperial urge was failing. Everyone knew what had been lost in the war that Kipling had so lauded as a cleansing force, but what had been gained?

The hated Liberals won a landslide election at the beginning of 1906 – as far as Kipling was concerned it was the end of imperial progress, particularly in South Africa where the new government was willing to restore self-government to the former Boer republics. For what, therefore, had the war been fought? Kipling's friend Jameson lost his majority in 1907 to be replaced by a Boer as Premier of the Cape Colony in 1908. The Union of South Africa, set up the following year as a dominion under the Crown, elected the former Boer general Louis Botha as Prime Minister in 1910.

The period of 1906 to 1914 was a bad one for the Conservatives. Liberals such as Winston Churchill and Lloyd George were redefining the social conditions of Britain and if the House of Lords were to get in their way, the House of Lords would also be redefined. Kipling became a one-man literary trouble-shooter for the nation, rushing from one issue to another – industrial unrest, the Balkan crisis, Ulster separatism, the German threat and military conscription.

His contributions were predictable and conducive to neither literature nor effective politics. Some of his intemperate statements reduced his public stature, such as in a widely reported speech on a common in Tunbridge Wells (a rare example of his public speaking) when he denounced the government as *a firm of fraudulent solicitors which have got an unlimited power of attorney from a client by false pretences and could dispose of their client's estate how they pleased.*[191] The speech was reprinted by the *Daily Express* and sold at a penny a page to assist women refugees who were supposedly to flood out of Ulster on Irish independence.

With weary inevitability, Kipling opposed the movement for women's suffrage on supposedly principled grounds. In fact there had been a majority in the House of Commons for some measure of women's franchise since the 1890s; the question by 1911 was which franchise measure would be chosen, one which best benefited the Conservatives or the Liberals. Clearly this was a battle of politics, not principle; the militancy of the suffragettes was an expression of frustration at government inaction in the face of the overwhelming moral case for female enfranchisement.

The suffragette campaign certainly succeeded in polarising opinion on the issue. Kipling's contribution was the poem that gave him one of his most famous lines in 'The Female of the Species'. As usual with Kipling, his literary abilities outstripped his limited political understanding and he produced a more complex piece than he seemingly intended. In a celebration of female strength he underlines male weakness:

> Man's timid heart is bursting with the things he must
>   not say ...
> Fear, or foolishness, impels him, ere he lay the wicked
>   low
> To concede some form of trial even to his fiercest foe.
> Mirth obscene diverts his anger – Doubt and Pity oft
>   perplex.

So the man is moved by uncertainty, sympathy and dirty jokes. On the other hand, the woman,

> She who faces Death by torture for each life beneath
>   her breast
> May not deal in doubt or pity – may not swerve for fact
>   or jest.

The notion is that because women have the imperative to bear children they are single-minded and merciless, and thus unsuited to politics. Quite apart from the fact that Kipling had long been decrying the lack of resolution among politicians, men also have a reproductive imperative, and if they can rise above biology to act judicially, there is no reason why women could not also do so.

Kipling sent it to his friend H A Gwynne, editor of

the right-wing *Morning Post*, who published it on 20 October 1911, ensuring a full post-bag for Kipling for weeks to come. In the Kipling household opinion was also divided: Carrie was opposed to the franchise being extended to women, while Elsie at 15 was in favour of women's political rights.

The family went to Canada in 1907 and Kipling was given his own Pullman car by the Canadian Pacific Railway, to hitch into any train going in his direction, or have shunted off to a siding when they wanted quiet. His resentment at his treatment in the US was still apparent when he wrote his memoirs 30 years later: *always the marvel – to which the Canadians seemed insensible – was that on one side of an imaginary line should be Safety, Law, Honour and Obedience, and on the other frank, brutal deci-vilisation.*[192] Kipling still would not cross that border to the US where his old home was a few hundred miles away; Carrie's mother instead made the trip north to see her daughter. Kipling was to maintain a connection with Canada through his friendship with Max Aitken, later Lord Beaverbrook, and Andrew Bonar Law, who was to become Conservative Prime Minster just before Kipling's cousin Stanley Baldwin did so in the early 1920s.

On their return to England, at the end of 1907, Kipling was told he had been awarded the Nobel Prize, the first time the award had been given to an English writer, which outraged those who confused his illiberal personal sentiments with his literature – a confusion which, to be fair, Kipling also made himself. He accepted the award but made no great fuss about it. His muted approach was echoed by the sombre mood in

Stockholm, for the old Swedish king died while Kipling and Carrie were sailing, and they found the city in mourning, in winter darkness for most of the day, and under snow. In consequence, many of the ceremonies connected with the prize-giving did not take place that year.

Kipling had always been severely subject to fevers and colds but after the age of 40, in 1905, his general health gave serious cause for concern. He stopped smoking in October 1908 on the advice of his doctor though resumed, perhaps not so heavily as previously.

Alice Kipling had been diagnosed as suffering from Graves' disease, a disorder of the thyroid the signs of which include fatigue, nervousness, emotional instability and irritability, which perhaps explains why Carrie found it difficult to deal with her husband's mother. Alice Kipling died at Tisbury on 23 November 1910, from heart failure, with Kipling, Trix and her husband present though Trix's mental health broke down again under the pressure, leaving Kipling to make all the arrangements. By the time Carrie arrived she said Trix was 'in a most excited and uncontrolled state.'[193] Lockwood, ailing and dispirited, lived a little longer but Kipling and Carrie were called back from holiday in Switzerland in January 1911 as his father had taken ill. He died of a heart attack before Kipling's arrival.

Other people of Kipling's parents' generation died around the same time: Aunt Aggie Poynter, Alfred Baldwin and Crom Price. Kipling found himself, in his 40s, at the gateway of life where there were as many people he loved dead as living, or perhaps more.

My Boy Jack

Kipling had shown a growing apprehension of Germany as the real enemy of the British Empire, at least since 1896 when the Kaiser had sent a telegram of support for the Boers after they had repulsed the disastrous Jameson Raid.

He had also, after his return from America in 1899, developed an association with the navy since they invited him to visit their ships in Dartmouth and Plymouth when he was living in Torquay. With his usual enjoyment of a man's world he settled into a relationship with sailors and ships which was personally rewarding if not greatly productive in literary terms. This gave him an understanding of the battle for naval supremacy in which Germany, already the dominant land power in Europe, aimed to rival Britain as the dominant sea power. Kipling was warning *The Teuton is angry, and is taking measures and steps as hard and fast as he can … The Teuton has his large cold eye on us …*[194]

In a personal reflection of Britain's relations with France, Kipling also found much to admire in neighbours across the Channel, making a particular friend of the uncompromising patriot Georges Clemenceau, twice Prime Minister of France, who visited Bateman's in September 1909 and remained a friend. At last Kipling had found a politician he could respect. Both were influenced by the Franco-Prussian war of 1870–1 in which France had been quickly overrun and accepted humiliating peace terms. The next war, it was widely believed, would be similarly fast and furious.

Kipling played no part in comment on or reaction to the events of summer 1914, leading to the war he had long predicted. He was still writing about Ulster as the primary flashpoint of political excitement in mid-July as the international crisis over Sarajevo developed. On 4 August 1914 Carrie noted in her diary she had a cold, Kipling wrote, *Incidentally Armageddon begins*.

When this long-prophesied war broke out he welcomed the national reaction with relief, *I confess I feel rather proud of the way in which England has bucked up at the pinch and tho', as you know, I am not an optimist by nature I can't help feeling cheerful over this.*[195]

The Boer War may have been a 'lesson' and it had its horrors, but for the British the majority of deaths were still, as they had been in previous wars, from disease caused by poor planning and inadequate sanitation. Kipling criticised this ill-preparedness but still regarded war, as it had been through his youth and most of the 19th century, as a sort of character-building adventure to make men out of boys.

Enthusiasm for the war caught the imagination of young men including John Kipling, a good-natured boy, not academic and with no particular abilities, who was destined for the services. He was sent away to St Aubyn's School, Rottingdean at the age of ten, presumably because it was felt boarding school values would do him some good. Kipling's letters to his son show a willingness to engage with emotional issues, even if the sentiments are conventional. He applauds John for facing homesickness with stoicism: *I understand that you did not flop about and blub and whine but carried on quietly. Good man! Next time it will come easier to you to keep control over yourself and the time after that easier still.* On the issue of homosexuality he warned John against, *any chap who is even suspected of beastliness ... Give them the widest of wide berths. Whatever their merits may be in the athletic line they are at heart only sweeps and scum and all friendship or acquaintance with them ends in sorrow and disgrace.*[196]

John was sent to Wellington College in Berkshire, which trained boys for Sandhurst. His lack of academic achievement suggested he would not pass the Sandhurst entrance exam so he went on to a private army crammer in Bournemouth in 1913. He was to have a career in the navy but his eyesight was too poor, so he tried for the army where the sight qualifications were lower. John had applied for a commission on 10 August 1914, in the first week of the war, and a week later Kipling took him to Maidstone for the physical examination but they *turned him down for eyes.*[197]

A story is told of how Kipling, accompanied by John, was helping to recruit volunteers outside the Bear public house in Burwash High Street when a neighbour, George Pagden, snapped, 'Why don't you send your own bloody boy?' The remark cut Kipling to the quick and he was said never to have set foot in the local village again.[198]

Kipling decided to pull strings and ask his old hero and acquaintance from India and South Africa, Lord Roberts, for a nomination. He met Roberts on 10 September at the Irish Guards HQ, whereupon the colonel of the regiment said John should report at once. Thus, with many attempts and only after pulling strings at the highest level, John Kipling was commissioned into the Irish Guards and told to report to Warley barracks on 14 September.

The family busied itself with war work: Carrie and Elsie sewing socks and Kipling visiting hospitals in the south of England and writing. He wrote two series of articles for the *Daily Telegraph*: 'The New Army in Training' and, after a visit to the Western Front in August 1915, 'France at War on the Frontier of Civilisation'. He was able to see some of the aftereffects of modern warfare with the countryside burned yellow for miles from a German gas attack, trees splintered into toothpicks and a ruined farm where no brick stood on another.

Kipling and his old school friend Dunsterville had been back in contact for some time. Dunsterville had not had the career Kipling had predicted for him; he had put in hard years in the Indian Army and was now a retired colonel. Once the war was in progress he was sent to India, to the north-west frontier then to the southern Caucasus, where his skeleton army Dunsterforce convinced the Turks by a series of tricks that a large army was present so they should not invade the Southern Caucasus in the wake of the Bolshevik Revolution. It was a truly Stalky-style moment at a time when there was little light relief.

The first phase of the war in 1914 followed the Schlieffen Plan for the German advance which had been in development for more than a decade when it was finalised in 1905. It involved the violation of Belgian neutrality as a key element; the armies would sweep through Belgium and knock out France in a swift blow.

In the event, fierce resistance from the Belgian population held back the advance, to which the Germans responded with the destruction of property and the execution of civilians, intended to cow the population. This behaviour was exaggerated into widespread atrocity stories which were used to stimulate the British population into war-fever.

Britain entered the war from a treaty obligation to guarantee Belgian neutrality, and in defence of the French ally. Before the end of 1914 stalemate had set in with the armies facing each other across a 365-mile line of trenches from the Swiss border to the coast. The great offensives of the following years, including at Loos in 1915, were attempts to break the deadlock.

The excitement of war stimulated the last great burst of creativity in Kipling's life. The first, published in *The Times*, was a call to arms written in the first weeks of war:

> *For all we have and are,*
> *For all our children's fate,*
> *Stand up and take the war.*
> *The Hun is at the gate!*

When Belgian refugees began to flood into Britain telling of the German advance, Kipling adopted a more grim tone with 'The Beginnings':

It was not part of their blood,
It came to them very late
With long arrears to make good
When the English began to hate.

Kipling's letters showed him much moved by tales of atrocities allegedly committed by the Germans as they crossed a fiercely resisting Belgium. A story on this theme, 'Swept and Garnished', has an elderly German woman with a fever visited by the ghosts of Belgian children killed by the German army.

A story with far greater depth was 'Mary Postgate', also written in 1915, where a spinster brings up and seemingly falls in love with her employer's nephew, despite his contemptuous treatment of her. He joins the Flying Corps and dies on a training flight. Mary is given the task of burning his things and as she does so, a child is killed in the village. It is suggested she was hit by a bomb dropped by a German aeroplane, though the doctor involved says it was a rotten stable beam which broke and threw debris down, hitting the child. He makes a point of telling Mary this, when she calls in to the village to get fuel for her bonfire, as he knows that in the fog of war it will be assumed that any unexpected death was caused by the Germans.

The beastliness of war and of the Germans is not stressed; it is Mary's employer and her nephew who are unpleasant, and the unrequited love of Mary for the young flyer is repeated incessantly. While Mary is burning the young man's possessions she sees a German airman who has fallen from a plane and is trapped, injured, in a tree nearby. She lets him die, enjoying *her long plea-sure* in a scarcely veiled sexual description where she vigorously stokes the fire and brings herself to a climax: *an increasing rapture laid hold on her. She ceased to think. She gave herself up to feel … She closed her eyes and drank it in … 'Go on' she murmured half aloud. 'That isn't the end.' Then the end came very distinctly in a lull between two rain-gusts. Mary Postgate drew her breath short between her teeth and shivered from head to foot.*

At the end of the story she goes home and has a hot bath. There is no external evidence to suggest there ever really was an airman; all we see is Mary's perception as she curses the 'pagan' hanging in the tree while she excites herself in front of the pyre on which burn the last remains of her unrequited love. She has been freed by the atmosphere of war to unleash those passions that a bourgeois life of self-restraint has kept bottled up within her.

Even at this stage in the national drama, in many ways the culmination of Kipling's imperial mission when the Empire must succeed or fail on the character of its men, Kipling had to create something bigger than himself. Mary Postgate, perhaps the finest fiction to come out of the First World War, is written as if it were driven by something stranger and more profound than Kipling's conscious thought.

Why we died

The family often visited John in London, sending the Rolls Royce to his barracks and the four of them going to the theatre. It was not something the parents usually did, but was much to the taste of John and Elsie.

There is no doubt that John wanted to get to war and brought a degree of boyish enthusiasm to the task. Kipling wrote that as he had toiled to make life pleasant for his children, he resented the shadow over his children's lives, but the young went to war with passion.

John was not sent directly to the front; he first served in Dublin then waited impatiently in London while his friends were dispatched. Finally he was sent forward into what would be known as the Battle of Loos, the British wing of the autumn offensive (the French attacked simultaneously in Champagne).

John Kipling's last thoughts were represented in 26 letters to his parents starting 'Dear Old Things' on Monday 16 September 1915. 'I am writing this in a train proceeding to the firing line at 15 mph (its top speed) ... we are billeted in a splendid little village nestling among the downs about 20 miles from the firing line ... the country is looking awfully nice.'

Later the going was harder: 'Never in my life have I seen rain like this the roads are flooded, there are feet of mud. The heavy firing has brought this on it hasn't stopped for two days ... 'His final letter, dated 25 September, reads: 'Just a hurried line as we start off tonight, the front line trenches are nine miles off from here so it won't be a very long march. This is the great effort to break through and end the war ... Funny to think one will be in the thick of it tomorrow and one's first experience of shell fire not in the trenches but in the open.'[199]

The Kiplings were all at Bateman's when they received a telegram from the war office on 2 October to say John was 'missing'. As they were to find out by slow and painful enquiry over the following months, he had been among the leading companies advancing in the Battle of Loos. John was firing his revolver when he was shot through the head, seriously wounding him, and he was laid under cover in a shell hole. The Germans then drove the British troops back and it was years before the spot where he had been laid was back in British hands. He was one of thousands reported missing in this battle alone.

The Kiplings made enquiries via neutral channels, American and Swiss officials, and Carrie was 'busy at my desk with correspondence about John's men and the hope of finding something, from the wounded men.' They toured hospitals on the South Coast where the wounded had been taken. By 15 October Carrie was writing, 'Seven weeks to the day since John was last seen and still no news. Constant and steady investigation has gone on and always we just miss seeing the man who could tell us.'[200]

Kipling wrote 'My Boy Jack' about this sad quest:

> 'Have you heard news of my boy Jack?'
> Not this tide
> 'When d'you think that he'll come back?'
> Not with this wind blowing, and this tide.

Kipling accepted John's death as a fact in a way in which Carrie perhaps never did. He wrote stoically to Lionel Dunsterville, *It was a short life. I'm sorry that all the years work ended in that one afternoon but – lots of people are in our position and it's something to have bred a man.*[201]

As usual, in his grief Kipling refused to talk and avoided reminders of John.

Kipling once asked exactly how much older Haggard was than himself. Haggard said ten years and Kipling replied, *Then you have the less time left in which to suffer*. Haggard considered his friend was speaking of the death of their sons. 'John's death has hit him very hard,' he wrote, 'I pointed out that this love of our lost sons was a case of what is called "Inordinate affection" in the Prayer Book. *"Perhaps"* he answered, *"but I do not care for ordinate affection."'*[202]

Another close observer of Kipling, D C Ponton, Elsie's teacher and occasionally (in the holidays) that of John from 1911 to 1914, saw him soon after John had been posted as 'wounded and missing'. 'Mr Kipling had no inclination to appeal for sympathy. All he said was, *"The boy had reached the supreme moment of his life, what would it avail him to outlive that?"* and the father concentrated himself not on revenge but on writing words that would comfort the bereaved and warn the world against making too easy conditions with a ruthless enemy.'[203] All family events were now overshadowed by the shade of the missing boy. On 2 February 1917 Elsie's 21st birthday was reported as, 'A quiet coming of age and all the coming of age we shall have in our little family now.'[204]

Kipling continued with non-fiction writing about the men and machines in war. He wrote *Sea Warfare* in 1916, a compilation of articles on the navy, and in 1917 started work on a history of the Irish Guards in the war. It was obviously a long homage to his son, via the lives of the men with whom he served, but the two volumes, published in 1923, were also a return to a more balanced attitude to the Southern Irish. Kipling had enjoyed his Irish character Private Mulvaney but by the time of the Ulster crisis before the war began, he was speaking of them as if they were virtually sub-human. The regimental history, full of anecdotes and colourful language, restores warmth and humanity to his vision of Catholic Ireland. It could easily be remarked that a regimental history did not need a literary genius to write it, but this is to miss the point: Kipling needed the book for it meant his house was often visited by young men of John's age who came to talk of the regiment and their experiences. Finishing the book was another kind of sadness for Kipling.

Oliver Baldwin (Stanley's son), who had been at school with John, later remarked that the war had provided a tragedy that changed Kipling from a great human being to a man with great sorrow. 'He was proud his son had joined the army at the age of 17. Here his inferiority complex had come out – he was not able to be a soldier himself, but his son was in uniform.' When John went missing, 'from that date Kipling became an entirely different man … It broke him completely. He shut up like a clam. All his creation went. He was not interested in creating anything new. All the lovely side of his nature – all the "Jungle Book", all the playing with children, all the love for people – went like that. He concentrated himself in revenge.' Baldwin said Kipling looked to him to avenge John, 'He wanted me to take his son's place, so that he would have somebody connected with him fighting.'[205]

Kipling had never shown much restraint in writing about the Germans; now the death of his son sent him into a welter of lunatic theorising. He tried to connect up the pacifists, socialists and anyone who felt there should be a negotiated peace by claiming that they were all covert masochists and they yearned for the overt sadism of the Germans. Germans, of course, were constitutionally wicked: *The one certain note of the German character under stress, is its unfailing beastliness and its use of certain well known forms of perversion and degeneracy.* As for the pacifist, German atrocities stimulated *a certain perverted interest.* Thus both the Germans prosecuting the war and the British wanting an end to the war without outright victory were sexual perverts.[206] Once again, as in 'Mary Postgate', Kipling conceives of the war through the metaphor of the unleashing of dark desires, best kept concealed, an indication of his own feelings as he struggled through the overwhelming challenges of the time.

Kipling's delight in the persecution of long-naturalised citizens of German extraction can only be explained in terms of mental imbalance. He described, for example, in September 1918 how *a party of Huns – dog and three dry bitches* (in fact an elderly invalid man and three old women) were chased out of their home overlooking the sea by a lynch mob on the premise that they signalled to the enemy and congratulated each other when dead British seamen were washed ashore.[207] It is indicative of Kipling's mental disturbance that he was writing about this not to one of the hacks with whom he often corresponded but to Stanley Baldwin, then Financial Secretary to the Treasury. Most letters to politicians from people in that state of mind are immediately thrown in the waste paper bin.

He continued raging against the politicians even though the despised Lloyd George's coalition government of 1917 was winning the war, and now included his cousin Baldwin and his friend Bonar Law. Doubtless through his political connections, Kipling was invited in September 1917 to become one of the Imperial War Graves Commissioners. He drafted most of the public words found on war graves, including suggesting the use of a phrase from Ecclesiastes for the standard lapidary 'Their name liveth for evermore' and others such as that for unidentified remains: *A Soldier of the Great War Known unto God*. In terms of poetry, his output was now fragmentary and bitter. It is best characterised by Epitaphs, short poems – sometimes only two lines – that blamed politicians and civilian munitions workers for the slaughter.

'A Dead Statesman', for example, says

I could not dig: I dared not rob:
Therefore I lied to please the mob.
Now all my lies are proved untrue
And I must face the men I slew.
What tale shall serve me here among
Mine angry and defrauded young?

In what way, one might ask, were politicians more responsible for the war than imperialist poets or industrialists? What were the dead defrauded by? A dream of empire? The belief that it was ennobling to die for your country? The anticipation that the war would be short? Kipling seems to have moved beyond hatred of the Austro-Hungarians and the Germans, who might reasonably be considered prime movers in the war that began in August 1914. Any general condemnation of politicians could equally well be directed by the German or French dead against their own statesmen. Reason had completely departed Kipling, to be replaced by grief.

In an even more troubling verse couplet the dead say:

If any question why we died,
Tell them, because our fathers lied.

Yet who was the dead son and who the father in his particular case? Kipling seems to have had somewhere in his mind the shocking knowledge that merely hanging the Kaiser would not assuage war guilt: there was a wider responsibility for the illusions of youth and the sacrifice of 1914–18, and part of it was his.

Angry Last Years

After the war Kipling was reported as having lost his buoyant step. It was never to return, and he relied more than ever on Carrie. Charles Carrington described their relationship at this time: 'Visitors noticed that she habitually followed him about the room with her eyes. Not only did she guard his health; she opened his letters, dictated replies to the secretary, corresponded with the literary agent, managed the household, and eventually farmed the land, watching all expenditure with a prudent eye.'[208] It was said by locals that Carrie was too parsimonious, and she would have got more out of the estate had she put more into it.

Kipling was less than nine stone in weight in May 1918. He had already been subjecting himself to 'Overwork and over-smoking' at the beginning of the war.[209] At the time of John's death he began to suffer severe gastric problems which were to trouble him thereafter. All his teeth were removed in 1921, a 'treatment' much in fashion at the time, in the belief that infected teeth were the root of many problems, a notion favoured by Kipling's friend and doctor Bland-Sutton. It added to Kipling's suffering that he was taking inappropriate medicines until he was ill in France in 1933 and a French doctor saw and diagnosed a duodenal ulcer. Kipling was given appropriate diets but was too exhausted to undergo an operation, which could have relieved his pain years previously.

Carrie remarked that his nights in particular were dreadful, and he often did not sleep more than an hour and a half. He was frequently doubled up in pain, which he bore uncomplainingly, according to Elsie. He was convinced he had cancer, an idea which found expression in stories such as 'A Madonna of the Trenches' and 'The Wish House' in which cancer plays a central role. In 'The Wish House' a woman takes on the pain of another, a man who has deserted her. The pain, she feels, *must* have a meaning. In the companion poem Kipling visualises

> *Mornings of memory, noontides of agony, midnights*
> *unslaked for her,*
> *Till the stones of the streets of her Hells and her*
> *Paradise ached for her.*
> *So she lived while her body corrupted upon her.*

Kipling had an unproductive operation on his stomach in late 1922 and thereafter a great deal of time was spent travelling in search of a healing climate. He and Carrie often visited France, where he had become something of a national hero, and which came to take the place in his affections previously filled by South Africa.

Kipling's illness gave Carrie added justification for her obsessive protection of him but her brooding presence was wearying to him and he delighted in having visitors living in Bateman's to relieve the boredom. 'My mother introduced into everything she did, and even permeated the life of her family with, a sense of strain and worry amounting sometimes to hysteria,' Elsie wrote. 'Her possessive and rather jealous nature, both with regard to my father and to us children, made our lives very difficult, while her uncertain moods kept us apprehensively on the alert for possible storms.'[210]

Elsie declared her intention to marry George Bambridge, a former officer of the Irish Guards, now a diplomat. It was not easy for the Kiplings to accept the loss of their last surviving child; Kipling was reported to be jealous of Bambridge and Carrie never reconciled herself to the fact that her daughter was a married woman, and she was constantly interfering in Elsie's life. The wedding, with a reception for 400, was held at St Margaret's, Westminster. At the end of the day Carrie wrote, 'We sadly return to face an empty side to our life and for the present are too weary to meet it.'[211] As for Kipling, 'Something like despair filled him as he looked forward to life at Bateman's without his only remaining child.'[212]

Though they rarely met, Kipling was sorry to lose his correspondent Theodore Roosevelt in 1919, and he wrote the poem 'Great-Heart' to honour him. Roosevelt had somewhat taken the place of Rhodes as Kipling's heroic man of vision and action. It says a good deal about the continuing traits in Kipling's character that even in his fifties, when he was one of the most famous men in the world, he still needed a hero to worship. Inevitably, after the coup by Mussolini in Italy in 1922 he began to speak positively of the fascist for his suppression of strikes and left-wing opponents, *a strong man ruling alone*, just the sort of character Kipling thought admirable.[213]

Kipling moved further towards the right under the influence of people such as Gwynne, editor of the *Morning Post* and Lady Bathurst, its proprietor, who nurtured the arrogance and insularity of the extremist in him. His extremism denying him adult political discourse, Kipling retreated into rage against his enemies and a conspiratorial anti-Semitism which was unworthy of him. He would write of the *'international Jew' at his worst* [214] but still had the newsman's sense to recognise the Protocols of the Elders of Zion, of which Gwynne sent him a copy, as a clumsy fake.

Before the war the Attorney-General Sir Rufus Isaacs, who had been implicated in the Marconi shares scandal, was appointed Lord Chief Justice by the Liberal government. Kipling wrote the vitriolic poem 'Gehazi', comparing Isaacs to the Biblical embezzler cursed by Elisha (2 Kings v 27). Of course, both curser and cursed in the original quotation were Jews, and Kipling's appropriation of a Biblical villain to point up a modern scandal is hardly anti-Semitic, though his fuming to Max Aitken (later Lord Beaverbrook) about *that Jew boy on the Bench* was.[215]

On the other hand, he wrote sympathetic poems in which he put himself in the role of Jewish characters, such as 'The Rabbi's Song' and 'The Song of Miriam Cohen', and recognised centuries of Jewish culture in 'The Treasure and the Law' in *Puck of Pook's Hill*.

Kipling might have felt some political satisfaction once Stanley Baldwin was Conservative prime minister, but no, *Stanley is a Socialist at heart* he said.[216]

In the public field the great writer's vision was utterly

defective. He continued to consider Lloyd George merely as a shifty and untrustworthy politician, though he had done more than any other Briton to win the war; and he despised and mistrusted Churchill though his views on the Empire and the danger from the Nazis were almost identical to Kipling's.

This was a sad end to a life of literary brilliance, but was all the sadder because Kipling's high level of invective against all his enemies had blunted his rhetoric and when he came to warn about the rise of the Nazis as a unique evil, no one believed him. Like a character from one of his own stories, he had squandered his reputation on inferior targets; when his country had need of a prophet of doom, his weapons were worn out.

Those who met Kipling at this time found his intensity disturbing and the emphases of his conversation inappropriate. The classicist Maurice Bowra met him with a group of young men, most of whom had been in the war and had no wish to talk about it but Kipling discussed it obsessively, lingering over the technical details of weapons. He then turned to politics, 'In which he seemed to dislike everyone and to think all British policies were wrong, and his language became coarser and cruder.' He urged severe punishment for the Germans, 'But what particularly exasperated him was Zionism. He called the Jews "Yids" and had nothing too bad to say about Arthur Balfour, who had been the successful advocate for a national home for the Jews in Palestine.' Kipling favoured the Arabs, and praised the Muslim troops in the Indian army, but 'he gave the impression that his views were formed less on reason than on hysterical emotions. Despite his courtesy, there was a note of violence in what he said, and I felt that fundamentally he was less sure of his opinions than he liked us to believe.'[217]

The extreme, uncontrolled nature of his passion is demonstrated by his reaction to southern Ireland gaining dominion status in 1921. 'Rud more depressed over the terms of South Ireland than he ever was during the War' Carrie wrote.[218] Yet Ulster had been maintained as part of the UK, something for which he had been arguing before the war. For Kipling to show such a reaction demonstrated his mind was unbalanced. His political preoccupations were still what they had been, but had gone over the edge where passion tumbles into madness. Kipling no longer had two sides to his head: the bigot had won over the aesthete.

When social and political disintegration did not follow the extension of the franchise to women over 30 in 1918, true to form, Kipling did not make a point of relenting on his previous views; and he grumbled when the Baldwin government gave women equal voting rights with men in 1928.

The novelist Hugh Walpole asked Kipling about *The Well of Loneliness* in 1928, when it was being prosecuted for obscenity for its far from explicit portrayal of lesbianism. Walpole, who may have been sounding out Kipling to support the defence, reported his opinion: 'No, he doesn't approve of the book. Too much of the abnormal in all of us to play about with it. Hates opening up reserves. All the same he'd had friends once and again he'd done more for than for any woman. Luckily Ma

Kipling doesn't hear this ... '[219] Perhaps for the reason that he did not wish to stir up 'the abnormal' in himself, Kipling did not deal with homosexuality in his work. This is despite his willingness to write of other contentious issues such as interracial sex, venereal disease, prostitution and marital violence.

Far from acting for the defence of Radclyffe Hall's book, the Home Secretary Sir Willam Joynson-Hicks persuaded Kipling to appear for the prosecution. Kipling wrote to the politician, *What I object to is its being sent to unmarried women. That gives the whole game away*.[220] Thus Kipling expresses an underlying theme of the anti-homosexual case: that reports of such sexual difference should be suppressed for fear the activities might seem too attractive to the sexually inexperienced and they would therefore be 'converted'. Kipling attended the appeal proceedings on 14 December 1928. In the event, literary evidence was not heard though Kipling supplied written evidence for the prosecution case in quotations from Juvenal and St Paul.

Last works

A series of miseries assailed Kipling in his final years. For the last 20 years of his life age and the constant pain of illness wore away at him. A man with such a sensitive awareness of his art must have long known that his gift was failing, but he kept producing work, if at a slower rate than previously.

It was nine years after his last collection, *A Diversity of Creatures* of 1917, before Kipling published a new set of stories, *Debits and Credits*, in 1926; his final collection, *Limits and Renewals*, was published six years after that, most of the pieces being in the elliptical, structurally complex late style which suggests an increase in artistry but a lack of vigour. The volume of stories produced was obviously lessened since his writing heyday in the 1890s and the stories show an obvious decline in quality with some exceptions born of recent experience such as 'The Gardener', about an unmarried mother whose son is killed in the war and whose grave she visits. This was stimulated by a visit Kipling and Carrie made in 1920 to the site of the Battle of Loos to trace John's last movements, unusual behaviour for Kipling whose normal reaction to grief was to shut it out.

The pressure of grief at John's death for Kipling was extreme, but worse than that was the failure of his mechanism for dealing with grief. After the death of Wolcott Balestier and Josephine Kipling he could order people not to speak about them and remove all reminders. He tried the same with John: the family were unable to go to Switzerland now, for its association with skiing holidays taken with John, and Kipling would not even have a bulldog in the house for it reminded him of his dead son's favourite pet. There was too much to shut out, however, after a death in such a public event as the war, when war memorials were being set up in every village in the country and Kipling was a War Grave Commissioner: he could not escape his grief.

In his sixties, much of Kipling's life became a reflection on the past rather than preparation for the future. On a visit to Southsea to inspect submarines Carrie noted in her diary, 'Rud takes me to see Lorne Lodge near St Bartholomew's Church and near Outram Road where he was so misused and forlorn and desperately unhappy as a child – and talks of it all with horror.'[221] While Carrie obviously knew of his literary depictions of the House of Desolation, this seems the first time he had talked to her about his experiences.

His principal literary projects in the early 1930s were the compilation and editing of *Collected Verse 1885–1932* and the preparation of the 35-volume Sussex Edition of his work. Now he laboured for the preservation of previous literary achievement, not new creation. The great pool of Kipling's talent was drying up in stages: first the poetry, then the fiction, leaving him with only his non-fiction writing and bibliographical work.

Approaching his 70th birthday, in 1935, he was working on his final book, a small classic of biography, *Something of Myself*, not published till 1937 after editing by Sir Alfred Webb-Johnson. It is indeed a partial autobiography: Kipling omits to comment on Flo Garrard, Edmonia Hill, Wolcott Balestier, his quarrel with Beatty; the death of Josephine and John Kipling; and he is curiously elliptical in mentioning Carrie. The omissions are of such magnitude that they give the biographer a guide to Kipling's life by default: anything really important to Kipling does not appear in his autobiography.

However, it has much fine writing and even at this late stage in his life it shows how Kipling still had a wonderful empathy with people and an ability to step inside the skin and see the world from the point of view of a black Pullman guard in Canada or a Swedish matron.

In his autobiography Kipling confided in the reader

how much of his work was seemingly motivated by a supernatural force. He wrote, *My Daemon was with me in the Jungle Books, Kim and both Puck Books, and good care I took to walk delicately, lest he should withdraw. I know that he did not, because when those books were finished they said so themselves with, almost, the waterhammer click of a tap turned off ... When your Daemon is in charge, do not try to think consciously. Drift, wait and obey.* [222]

While laying down instructions as to how his work was to be published, Kipling was ever wary of how others would perceive him and he did his utmost to circumscribe the biographers or practitioners of 'the higher cannibalism' as he often called them. He compulsively destroyed large amounts of family papers, including all his parents' correspondence, in what Trix later referred to 'the frenzy of burning any letters or papers connected with his youth (and mine too – alas!) which possessed him after mother's death.'[223]

Such behaviour seems like the action of a man desperate to conceal something but such an interpretation is open to question. Kipling had a general respect for privacy and therefore a belief that letters should be read only by the person for whom they are intended, not anyone else at whatever historical remove. Nor should mere professional standards be forgotten; he had the love of a professional for finished work. Kipling was a man who frequently threw work away or set it aside for months or years before resuming on it. Published pieces he relentlessly polished when he came to republish them in collections. A letter is of necessity a functional object which will not admit of much improvement. Anyone wanting to know of Lockwood Kipling, his son seemed to be saying, should look at the many examples of his finished work in India and Britain, not poke through his letters.

Carrie's health gave way at the beginning of the 1930s on a visit to the West Indies, with appendicitis added to the rheumatism and diabetes that plagued her. Kipling spent months in lodgings in Bermuda while she was in hospital.

Elsie had lived with her husband in his diplomatic postings in Brussels, Madrid and Paris where her parents had visited, until 1933 when the Bambridges returned to England. They stayed in a house in Hampstead where Kipling and Carrie visited them in early 1936 on their way to a holiday in France.

On the night of 9 January 1936 Kipling fell ill while staying at Brown's Hotel and was taken to the Middlesex Hospital. He was attended by a friend, surgeon Sir Alfred Webb-Johnson, who approached the ailing man's bedside and asked what was wrong. *Something has come adrift inside* said Kipling.[224] It was a perforated duodenum. He was operated on three days later but in his weakened state he could not recover. Carrie and Elsie were with him as he lost consciousness and ebbed away. The last entry in Carrie's diary, for 18 January 1936 reads: 'Rud died at 12.10am. Our Wedding Day.'

Kipling was cremated at Golders Green two days later. Incongruously, as the small party arrived for the ceremony, they heard the singing of 'The Red Flag' for the previous cremation had been that of Indian Communist Shapurji Saklatvala. Kipling would not have been amused. More to his taste would have been the ceremony in Westminster Abbey on 23 January when, to the sound of his 'Recessional' being sung, Kipling's ashes were interred in Poets' Corner. It was the day when George V's body was brought to London to lie in state, for the king had died on 20 January. There was a solemn appropriateness about the king-emperor and his great scribe ending their lives at the same time.

Conclusion

Kipling's complex internal life reflected itself in his work in a more subtle and allusive manner than is the case with most writers, which is presumably why he was so secretive about that life. It is that buried essence of himself that gives the answer to the question posed by Orwell at the beginning of this book: 'why it is that he survives while the refined people who have sniggered at him seem to wear so badly.'[225]

Kipling was below average height, extremely short-sighted and prone to illness but he loved swaggering about world literature in the company of tough men. When he actually encountered a tough man on the road in the form of Beatty Balestier he was unable to cope. His reaction to genuine threat was to run away rather than confront it, or, in the case of bereavement, not to speak of it.

Kipling was a tremendously well-travelled writer, yet it seemed he was cutting out parts of his life as tragedy was associated with different countries. He never returned to India, the country that made his name, after he was told while he was there that Wolcott Balestier was dead; after his daughter died in America he was never to return there; he removed from his house any reminder of dead children or friends. He kept the South African house, the Woolsack, loaned by his dead friend Rhodes, but would not visit the country again after Jameson lost the election and the Boers were in control.

Running away from conflict or denial of painful experiences may be unattractive traits for a person to have, but they were productive for Kipling, who internalised his difficulties and turned them into literature. Thus there is always the sense of buried truth with the best Kipling, that the story is not everything but the reader is reaching in the dark to understand more.

The process started when he was six when his experience of the House of Desolation gave him an instinctive understanding that he could only escape his torment by the creation of a fantasy world within. His childhood left him bereft, with a desperate urge to please older women, who were replacements for the mother who had abandoned him, but also a hero worship of men, filling the corresponding place of the missing father.

Kipling loved men and male company though he did not engage with them sexually; in that area he was attracted to older, masculine or lesbian women. This is not suggestive of homosexuality, it rather indicates that those who divide sexual feelings into merely homo- and hetero-sexuality are using too crude a scale. Sex is more interesting and has more to offer than that. In literary terms, Kipling's sexuality is a key to his extraordinary ability to understand the feelings of middle-aged women, a gift he displayed in characters from Mrs Hauksbee to Mary Postgate. With men he communicated, to less beneficial literary effect, by talking about technology or politics.

When he approached the inner child, however, it

was as if he entered a different world. His children were often under six, the age at which he was placed in the House of Desolation; or just under puberty, the age at which he was released. They inhabit two worlds: European and Indian; human and animal; or historical and present day. Kipling's gift dwindles as the children grow up, and he has little to say to adolescents.

Kipling gives a sense of having been set apart from society by his unique experiences, which produced an individual creed. His best characters live by a set of rules, explicitly set out in the Law of the Jungle but implicit in the behaviour of his best characters. Thus in 'The Record of Badalia Herodsfoot' Badalia takes money from the church to do social work, which is just but far from Christian. She accepts murderous violence from her drunken husband but would never give him away to the police any more than the Soldiers Three would report misconduct. The boys in *Stalky & Co* would tie up and torture another boy to 'teach him a lesson', but would not sneak to a master about him. Kipling may have been an authoritarian, but the authority was authority for other people. For himself, and for those he respected, the rules were personal. Authority had betrayed Kipling as a child, and he made up his own rules to live by; he was The Cat That Walked By Himself: doing deals with life on his own terms according to a personal creed.

He refused, therefore, to allow the pains of bereavement and defeat to touch him, yet the pressure of suppressed private grief released itself in his public anger at political targets. Many people mellow and are able to take a mature and longer view of the world in later life;

Kipling was one of those who did not. He became narrower in his outlook, more closed and unreceptive to new influences, at a cost to his reputation. The change was not immediate, but he got harder, his opinions ossified as he aged. Of course, he was thrown off balance by his own near-death and the death of his beloved daughter, as anyone would be. What was remarkable was his reaction: hurling himself into the morally dubious Boer War and a compulsive meddling in politics, a trade for which he had neither the necessary skills nor the temperament.

To witness Kipling repeatedly returning to the political fray is to recall his lines from 'The Gods of the Copybook Headings':

> ... the Dog returns to his Vomit and the Sow returns to
>   her Mire,
> And the burnt Fool's bandaged finger goes wabbling
>   back to the Fire.

Kipling had no ability to compromise or willingness to withhold comment until a more propitious time; no ability to set aside grudges and see the principle beyond the man. It is almost impressive to observe a man so keen to perform in the political arena, so little blessed with any skills that would aid him, and so unable to see it.

It is unfortunate for his position that he so tarnished his reputation, for most of the values Kipling espoused were universal and could be admired in any society, such as self-denial for the common good, bravery in the face of danger, and preparedness to resist attack. They became risible when they were endlessly repeated by the insincere and hypocritical – precisely those people who Kipling satirised in the Stalky stories.

On the negative side of his views, Kipling did stand for the self-deception of empire: presenting the illusion that it was operated in the interests of subject people; the empire builders laboured *to seek another's profit, / And work another's gain.* While this was not true (for the brown man's burden was markedly heavier than the white's) it is the case that the British Empire was well-run and was generally benign, particularly if compared to the Belgian, German or Japanese imperial presence. As Kipling predicted, the Empire faced its greatest challenge in the late 1930s when, incidentally, it was at its largest. The Second World War was a victory over racist authoritarians, after which democracy was successively restored in the states of western Europe, and former colonies were freed in a dismantling of foreign empires.

We are left, when most former British colonies have been independent for approaching half a century, with the fact that in terms of peace, law and order, transport, health or any other measure of a successful society, the British Empire was able to deliver while self-rule failed to do so, at least in the short term. Nor was the autocratic rule of the British replaced by resilient democracy in most places, with the honourable exception of India.

The departure from Empire was the largest largely peaceful handover of power in world history. It was not entirely without bloodshed, but when compared with France's ill-fated attempts to hang on to Algeria and

Vietnam, or Portugal's in Mozambique and Angola, Kipling's empire did very well in disbanding itself with a minimum of pain. The values of stoic pragmatism which had sustained empire also distinguished it in dissolution.

Kipling feared for the future of the Empire and its values. Had he a wider, deeper and longer vision he would have found more in the future to his liking. His views about such issues as women, homosexuality, 'a strong man ruling alone' and the position of the armed forces in society would find a better reception in African culture in the 21st century than in Britain.

Even in Europe and North America Kipling's work has done extraordinarily well for someone who is often thought of as a Victorian writer with outmoded imperialist views. His work ranges over such a wide field, and is so complex and allusive that there is always something for a new generation to grasp. Kipling's enduring images recur throughout literature, such as the airman dying suspended in a tree from 'Mary Postgate' which reappears in Golding's 1954 classic *Lord of the Flies*. The Walt Disney production of *The Jungle Book*, made in 1967, has introduced the basic theme and characters of the work to successive generations, in one of the most successful children's films ever made. The Jungle Book as a cartoon was of necessity changed by Disney (and it was the last film he personally oversaw) but the central metaphor of the man raised by wolves, the character of his ambiguous life and the cast of animals is so strong as to shine through this treatment.

Lindsay Anderson's *If ... .* as well as taking its title

(with the addition of four dots) from Kipling, took the school study life of *Stalky & Co* and pushed it into an anarchic 1968. In this he replicated the way in which Kipling had remoulded the improving public school stories of Dean Farrer's *Eric or Little by Little*.

A line adapted from the poem 'The Ladies', 'sisters under the skin', was adopted as a motto in the 1970s and 1980s by feminist separatists who thought, as Kipling did, that gender was more important than class or education. On a similar theme, the emotionally charged sex war of *The Light that Failed* has stayed in print, to be read now as a study in pathology, of the 'old' man rendered impotent by the New Woman, a key text in gender studies.

Kipling's influence has been particularly widespread in former colonies. It was very noticeable while writing this book that of the librarians, journalists and others I came into contact with in London, it was black people with roots in other countries who wanted to talk about Kipling and spoke of his work with affection. For the whites he was just another Dead White European Male in the literary canon. For those who came from Commonwealth countries, Kipling was one of the few canonical writers who had something to say about what gave them the lives they have. Kipling the literary chameleon is still crossing barriers.

Notes

Edition details are given for longer works but it would be otiose to reference each short story or poem where the derivation is clearly indicated in the main text and there have been so many editions.

KP refers to the Kipling Papers, housed in the Kipling Archive at the University of Sussex.

1 Kipling, Rudyard, *Something of Myself* (Penguin, London 1977) p 111
2 Orwell, George, in a review of 'A Choice of Kipling's Verse', *Horizon* (February 1942)
3 Birkenhead, Lord, *Rudyard Kipling* (Weidenfeld and Nicolson, London 1978) p 12
4 *Something*, p 8
5 *Something*, p 7
6 *Something*, p 9
7 *Something*, p 10
8 *Something*, p 11
9 Kipling, 'Baa Baa Black Sheep'
10 *Something*, p 17
11 *Something*, p 18
12 *Something*, p 17
13 *Something*, p 18
14 *Something*, p 19
15 Kipling, 'School Song'
16 *Something*, p22
17 *Something*, p 22

18 Beresford, G C in Orel, Harold, *Kipling Interviews and Recollections* (Totowa, New Jersey 1983) vol 1, p 35

19 *Something*, p 26

20 Birkenhead, *Kipling*, p 41

21 Birkenhead, *Kipling*, pp 50–1

22 Fleming, Trix, KP 32/32

23 Fleming, Trix, to Mrs Bambridge 15 June 1940, KP 32/24

24 Birkenhead, *Kipling*, p 50

25 Fleming, Trix, KP 32/32

26 *Something*, p 34

27 *Something*, p 34

28 Fleming, Trix, KP 32/32

29 *Something*, p 35

30 *Something*, p 38

31 Pinney, Thomas (ed) *The Letters of Rudyard Kipling*, vol 1 (Palgrave Macmillan, London 1990) p 57

32 Birkenhead, *Kipling*, p 72

33 Pinney, *Letters*, vol 1, pp 107–9

34 Page, Norman, *A Kipling Companion* (Palgrave Macmillan, London 1984) pp 185–6

35 Birkenhead, *Kipling*, p 63

36 *Something*, p 44

37 Carrington, Charles, *Rudyard Kipling, His Life and Work* (Penguin, London 1955) p 113

38 *Something*, p 46

39 Birkenhead, *Kipling*, p 69

40 Pinney, Thomas, *Something of Myself and Other Autobiographical Writings* (Cambridge University Press, Cambridge 1990) p 174

41 Fleming, Trix, in Orel, *Interviews and Recollections*, vol 1, pp 4, 12

42 Pinney, *Letters*, vol 1, p 80

43 Pinney, *Letters*, vol 1, p 106

44 Birkenhead, *Kipling*, p 75

45 Carrington, *Kipling*, p 101

46 Robinson, E Kay, in Orel, *Interviews and Recollections*, vol 1, pp 68, 71

47 Kipling, R, in Orel, *Interviews and Recollections*, vol 1, pp 59–60

48 Pinney, *Letters*, vol 1, p 140

49 Kipling, 'Three and – an Extra'

50 Pinney, *Letters*, vol 1, p 103

51 Pinney, *Letters*, vol 1, p 39

52 Pinney, *Letters*, vol 1, p 178

53 Pinney, *Letters*, vol 1, p 111

54 Pinney, *Letters*, vol 1, p 133

55 Pinney, Thomas, *Something of Myself and Other Autobiographical Writings*, pp 210–11. Harry Ricketts' interpretation of the diary entries is followed here.

56 Hill, Edmonia, in Orel, *Interviews and Recollections*, vol 1, p 92

57 Lang, Andrew, from *Essays in Little* (1891) reprinted in Green, Roger Lancelyn (ed), *Kipling The Critical Heritage* (Routledge and Kegan Paul, London 1971) p 73

58 Younghusband, Major-General Sir George, *A Soldier's Memories In Peace and War* (Herbert Jenkins, London 1917) pp 187–8

59 Carrington, *Kipling*, p 152

60 *Something*, p 52

61 *Something*, p 53

62 Pinney, *Letters*, vol 1, p 216

63 Hill, Edmonia, in Orel, *Interviews and Recollections*, vol 1, p 203

64 Hill, Edmonia, in Orel, *Interviews and Recollections*, vol 1, p 205

65 Kipling, Rudyard, *From Sea to Sea* (Doubleday and McClure, New York 1899) vol 1, p 439

66 Carrington, *Kipling*, p 175

67 Baetzhold, Howard G, in Orel, *Interviews and Recollections*, vol 1, p 154

68 *Something*, p 63

69 Fleming, Trix, KP 32/32

70 Pinney, *Letters*, vol 1, p 354

71 Pinney, *Letters*, vol 1, p 378

72 Birkenhead, *Kipling*, p 91

73 Lang, Andrew, in Green, *The Critical Heritage*, p 71

74 'Anon' [Barry Pain], *Cornhill Magazine*, October 1890, p 367

75 Pinney, *Letters*, vol 1, p 356

76 Pinney, Thomas (ed), *The Letters of Rudyard Kipling*, vol 2 (Palgrave Macmillan, London 1990) p 9

77 Carrington, *Kipling*, p 179

78 Hooper, CF, in Orel, *Interviews and Recollections*, vol 1, p 116

79 Birkenhead, *Kipling*, p 112

80 Low, Sidney, in Orel, *Interviews and Recollections*, vol 1, pp 119, 121

81 Lewis Hind, C, in Orel, *Interviews and Recollections*, vol 1, p 128

82 Peacock, Roger, in Orel, *Interviews and Recollections*, vol 1, p 138

83 Hooper, C F, in Orel, *Interviews and Recollections*, vol 1, p 116

84 Birkenhead, *Kipling*, p 109

85 Kipling, Rudyard, *The Light that Failed* (London 1891) pp 56–7

86 Fleming, Trix, KP 32/32

87 Fleming, Trix, KP 32/32

88 Kipling, TLTF, p 70

89 Fleming, Trix, KP 32/32

90 Kipling, TLTF, p 74

91 Kipling, TLFT, p 57

92 Kipling, TLTF, p 68

93 Kipling, TLTF, p 191

94 Carrington, Kipling, in the 1978 reprinting of the 1955 biography, p 613

95 Carrington, Kipling, p 217. Beerbohm was writing about a 1903 stage dramatisation of the book. It has been filmed four times, in 1914, 1916, 1923 and 1939.

96 Kipling, TLTF, p 121

97 Pinney, Letters, vol 2, p 19

98 James, Henry, in Green, The Critical Heritage, p 68

99 Gosse, Edmund, in Green, The Critical Heritage, p 116

100 Bookman review in Green, The Critical Heritage, p 134

101 Ricketts, Harry, The Unforgiving Minute: A Life of Rudyard Kipling (London 1999) p 167

102 Birkenhead, Kipling, p 51

103 The Times, 3 February 1938, p 14

104 Pinney, Letters, vol 2, p 26

105 Carrington, Kipling, p 228

106 Birkenhead, Kipling, p 117

107 Stoddard, Charles Warren, in Orel, Kipling Interviews and Recollections, vol 2 (Totowa, New Jersey 1983) p 219

108 Birkenhead, Kipling, p 116

109 Carrington, Kipling, p 239

110 Carrington, Kipling, p 241

111 Pinney, Letters, vol 2, pp 44–5

112 Kipling, R and Balestier, Wolcott, *The Naulahka* (London 1892) pp 262, 275

113 Kipling, R, *Letters of Travel 1892–1913* (New York 1920) p 5

114 *Something*, p 83

115 *Something*, pp 84–5

116 *Something*, p 85

117 *Something*, p 87

118 *Carrie's Diaries*, KP, 11 November 1893

119 *Pinney, Letters*, vol 2, p 153

120 Allen, Charles (ed) *Kipling's Kingdom* (London 1987) p 41

121 Matthews, Brander in Green, *The Critical Heritage*, p 338

122 *Pinney, Letters*, vol 1, p 378

123 *Carrie's Diaries*, KP, 31 December 1893

124 *Pinney, Letters*, vol 2, p 129

125 *Birkenhead, Kipling*, p 153

126 Anonymous, in Orel, *Kipling*, vol 2, p 202

127 Stoddard, Charles Warren, in Orel, *Kipling* vol 2, p 211

128 *Pinney, Letters*, vol 2, p 210

129 *Birkenhead, Kipling*, p 164

130 *Carrie's Diaries*, KP, 5 April 1895

131 Van de Water, Frederick F, in Orel, *Interviews and Recollections*, vol 2, p 220. All direct quotation from Beatty is from this source.

132 *Birkenhead, Kipling*, p 162

133 Van de Water, Frederick F, in Orel, *Interviews and Recollections*, vol 2, p 223

134 *Birkenhead, Kipling*, p 166

135 *Carrie's Diaries*, KP, 23 February 1896

136 *Pinney, Letters*, vol 2, p 240

137 *Pinney, Letters*, vol 2, p 245

138 Carrington, *Kipling*, p 299

139 Birkenhead, *Kipling*, p 174

140 Wells, H G, *The Outline of History* (London 1920) reprinted in Green, *The Critical Heritage*, p 307

141 Buchanan, Robert, reprinted in Green, *The Critical Heritage*, p 244

142 Facsimile in *Kipling Papers*

143 Besant, Sir Walter, reprinted in Green, *The Critical Heritage*, p 257

144 Fleming, Trix, in Orel, *Interviews and Recollections*, vol 1, p 132

145 Pinney, *Letters*, vol 2, p 337

146 *Something*, p 112

147 *Something*, p 130

148 Pinney, *Letters*, vol 2, p 339

149 Pinney, *Letters*, vol 2, p 354

150 Carrington, *Kipling*, p 345

151 Pinney, *Letters*, vol 2, p 350

152 *Carrie's Diaries, KP*, 23 February 1899

153 Garland, Hamlin, in Orel, *Interviews and Recollections*, vol 2, p 258

154 Carrington, *Kipling*, p 349

155 Birkenhead, *Kipling*, p 197

156 *Carrie's Diaries, KP*, 5 March 1899

157 Garland, Hamlin, in Orel, *Interviews and Recollections*, vol 2, p 258

158 Pinney, *Letters*, vol 2, p 376

159 Thirkell, Angela, in Orel, *Interviews and Recollections*, vol 2, p 311 and Fleming, Trix, KP 32/34

160 Pinney, *Letters*, vol 2, p 376

161 Pinney, Thomas (ed), *The Letters of Rudyard Kipling*, vol 3 (Palgrave Macmillan, London 1996) p 10

162 *Something*, p 113

163 *Pinney, Letters, vol 3, p 5*

164 *Something, pp 113–14*

165 *Something, p 115*

166 *Pinney, Letters, vol 3, pp 41–2*

167 *Something, p 124*

168 *Pinney, Letters, vol 3, p 53*

169 *Younghusband, Major-General Sir George, A Soldier's Memories In Peace and War (London 1917) p 189*

170 *Pinney, Letters, vol 3, p 87*

171 *Birkenhead, Kipling, p 232*

172 *Pinney, Letters, vol 3, p 6*

173 *Something, p 105*

174 *Rogers, Joseph M, in Orel, Interviews and Recollections, vol 2, p 195*

175 *Edel, Leon (ed), The Henry James Letters, vol 4, 1895–1916 (Cambridge, Mass. 1984) pp 210–11*

176 *Pinney, Letters, vol 3, p 11*

177 *The polished version from The Works of Rudyard Kipling is used, which shows slight differences from the version in Kim and is expanded by another three stanzas*

178 *Carrie's Diaries, KP, July–August 1901*

179 *Bambridge, Elsie, 'Memoir' in Carrington, Kipling, p 592*

180 *Jerome, Jerome K, in Orel, Harold, Kipling: Interviews and Recollections (Totowa, New Jersey 1983) vol 1, p 157*

181 *Lockwood Kipling quoting his son in Carrington, Kipling, p 437*

182 *Hill, Edmonia, in Orel, Interviews and Recollections (Totowa, New Jersey 1983) vol 1, p 93*

183 *Pinney, Letters, vol 3, p 149*

184 *Chesterton, G K, in Green, The Critical Heritage, p 273*

185 *Something, p 138*

186 Young, A B Filson, *The Complete Motorist* (London 1904) p 286

187 *Something*, p 142

188 Pinney, *Letters*, vol 3, p 424

189 Carrington, *Kipling*, p 451

190 Ricketts, Harry, *The Unforgiving Minute: A Life of Rudyard Kipling* (London 1999) p 283

191 *The Times*, 1 May 1914

192 *Something*, p 149

193 Carrie's Diaries, KP, 25 November 1910

194 Birkenhead, *Kipling*, p 252

195 Pinney, Thomas (ed), *The Letters of Rudyard Kipling*, vol 4 (Palgrave Macmillan, London 1999) p 250

196 Gilbert, Eliot L, '*O Beloved Kids*' *Rudyard Kipling's Letters to his Children* (London 1984) pp 46, 127

197 Pinney, *Letters*, vol 4, p 251

198 I am grateful to Michael Lacy, a National Trust guide at Bateman's, for this anecdote.

199 Letters from John Kipling, KP, 32/2

200 Carrie's Diary, KP, 15 & 18 October 1915

201 Pinney, *Letters*, vol 4, p 345

202 Rider Haggard, Lilias, *The Cloak That I Left* (Hodder and Stoughton, London 1951) reprinted in Orel, *Interviews and Recollections*, vol 1, pp 149–50

203 D C Ponton, KP, 32/6

204 Carrie's Diary, KP, 2 February 1917

205 *Daily Telegraph*, 29 July 1936

206 Pinney, *Letters*, vol 4, pp 419–20

207 Pinney, *Letters*, vol 4, p 511

208 Carrington, *Kipling*, p 523

209 Carrie's Diary, KP, 26 June 1914

210 Bambridge, Elsie, 'Memoir' in Carrington, *Kipling*, p 592

211 *Carrie's Diary, KP, 22 October 1924*

212 *Bambridge, Elsie, 'Memoir' in Carrington, Kipling, p 596*

213 *Birkenhead, Kipling, p 300*

214 *Birkenhead, Kipling, p 290*

215 *Pinney, Letters, vol 4, p 208*

216 *Birkenhead, Kipling, p 301*

217 *Bowra, C M, Memories 1898–1939 (Weidenfeld and Nicolson, London 1966) pp 188–9*

218 *Carrie's Diary, KP, 7 December 1921*

219 *Hart-Davis, Rupert, Hugh Walpole (Hamilton, London 1985) p 297*

220 *Lycett, Andrew, Rudyard Kipling (Weidenfeld and Nicolson,*
London 1999) p 551

221 *Carrie's Diary, KP, 25 February 1920*

222 *Something, p157*

223 *Trix Fleming to Elsie Bambridge, 15 June 1940, KP 32/24*

224 *Birkenhead, Kipling, p 357*

225 *Orwell, George, in a review of 'A Choice of Kipling's Verse', Horizon (February 1942)*

List of Works

There are many problems in attempting even a brief bibliography of Kipling. His work, particularly the writing of his youth, was subject to repeated and sometimes substantial revision. Magazine publication often preceded publication in volume form for novels, stories and poems so there are two dates of publication, or three if United States publication is included. There were also additions to volumes that had already been published. This is particularly obvious in collections of poetry. To take Departmental Ditties, published in 1886 in India, as an example: 'The Galley-Slave', Kipling's valediction to India, was not published as part of the volume until 1890, when he had already left the sub-continent. In this brief list the first publication of collections only is noted, with occasional necessary exceptions.

1881	*Schoolboy Lyrics (privately published)*
1886	*Departmental Ditties*
1888	*Plain Tales from the Hills*
1888	*The Indian Railway Library comprising the collections:*
	Soldiers Three
	The Story of the Gadsbys
	In Black and White
	Under the Deodars
	The Phantom Rickshaw
	Wee Willie Winkie

1890–91	*The Light that Failed* (novel) 12-chapter version US 1890 and UK 1891.
	15-chapter version 1891
1891	*Life's Handicap* (stories)
1892	*The Naulahka* (novel, with Wolcott Balestier)
1892	*Barrack-Room Ballads*
1893	*Many Inventions* (stories)
1894	*The Jungle Book*
1895	*The Second Jungle Book*
1896	*The Seven Seas* (verse)
1896	*Soldier Tales*
1897	*Captains Courageous* (novel)
1898	*The Day's Work* (stories)
1899	*Stalky & Co.*
1899	*From Sea to Sea* (two vols, travel)
1901	*Kim* (novel)
1902	*Just So Stories*
1903	*The Five Nations* (verse)
1904	*Traffics and Discoveries* (stories)
1906	*Puck of Pook's Hill* (stories)
1909	*Actions and Reactions* (stories)
1910	*Rewards and Fairies* (stories)
1911	*A School History of England* (history, with C R L Fletcher)
1912	*Songs from Books* (verse)
1917	*A Diversity of Creatures* (stories)
1919	*The Years Between* (verse)
1920	*Letters of Travel 1892–1913* (travel)
1923	*The Irish Guards in the Great War* (two vols, history)
1926	*Debits and Credits* (stories)
1930	*Thy Servant a Dog* (stories)
1932	*Limits and Renewals* (stories)
1937	*Something of Myself* (autobiography, published posthumously)

Further Reading

For someone who adjured posterity to seek not to question other than / The books I leave behind, Kipling has been extremely well served by biographers and continues to attract biographical interest.

Kipling's autobiography Something of Myself (first published by Macmillan, London 1937) is a good guide to the areas it covers such as his early life, life in India, first years of marriage and the Boer War, despite its many omissions.

There is the choice of not one but two authorised biographies, both by writers who had the advantage of being able to speak to people who knew Kipling intimately.

Though three writers were tried, Carrie Kipling failed to find a satisfactory biographer; and after her death Elsie Bambridge sought a biographer for her father's life. Her husband introduced her to another military man, Lord Birkenhead, who was hoping to make a name for himself as a biographer and who laboured on Kipling and Carrie's papers and interviewed people who had known Kipling well in Britain and the USA. When he presented a draft to Elsie in 1948 (significantly, after the death of Captain Bambridge in 1943) she forbade him to publish it, and sought another biographer.

The eventual official biographer was Charles Carrington, whose authorised biography, Rudyard Kipling: His Life and Work (first published by Macmillan, London) appeared in 1955. Birkenhead continued work on his own book, however. Birkenhead's son, after his father's death in 1976 (and Elsie's in 1975), felt free from the prohibition on publication and

Birkenhead's book came out in 1978 under the title *Rudyard Kipling* (Weidenfeld and Nicolson, London), subsequently published by other publishers.

Such biographical riches are matched with original source material in the form of the *Letters of Rudyard Kipling*, in six volumes (Palgrave Macmillan, London: 1990–2004) edited with erudite notation by Thomas Pinney. Harold Orel has collected two lively volumes of personal reminiscences of Kipling, published as *Kipling: Interviews and Recollections* (Macmillan, London: 1983).

Kipling has not been short of later interpreters. Angus Wilson's perceptive *The Strange Ride of Rudyard Kipling* (Secker and Warburg, London: 1977) gives a thoughtful analysis of why the man was so buttoned-down, challenging him with 'persistent evasion of introspection.' Martin Seymour-Smith, in *Rudyard Kipling* (Macdonald, London: 1989) writes what is really a long essay musing on Kipling's personal qualities of authoritarianism and homo-eroticism; and frankly calls him a 'repressed homosexual'.

In *The Unforgiving Minute* (Chatto and Windus, London: 1999) Harry Ricketts, also a poet, gives a detailed analysis of the way in which Kipling's life is closely reflected in his work. David Gilmour's exemplary *The Long Recessional: The Imperial Life of Rudyard Kipling* (John Murray, London: 2002) details the complexity of Kipling's relationship to the Empire and contemporary criticism of it.

Andrew Lycett's *Rudyard Kipling* (Weidenfeld and Nicolson, London: 1999) is the extensively researched, fully comprehensive, 659-page biography that brings up to date the work of the official biographers.

My constant companion in writing this biography has been Norman Page's *A Kipling Companion* (Macmillan, London: 1984), an invaluable fast guide to Kipling's life and work.

For general works on the great events in which Kipling took part: Thomas Pakenham's *The Boer War* (Weidenfeld and Nicolson, London: 1979) is the classic history of the conflict; and those interested in the Indian sub-continent's history during Kipling's lifetime could do worse than read Jad Adams and Phillip Whitehead's *The Dynasty: The Nehru-Gandhi Story* (Penguin, London: 1997).

The primary source for work on Kipling is the Kipling Archive at the University of Sussex, and I wish to thank the librarians there. Material from the Kipling Papers is used by kind permission of The National Trust. If any copyright has been created by the present publication of previously unpublished material, the author and publisher of *Kipling* unreservedly relinquish this in favour of The National Trust.

My thanks are due to Thomas Pinney for patiently answering queries. Quotations from his *Letters of Rudyard Kipling* are used with the permission of Palgrave Macmillan.

Quotations from Kipling's published work are used by permission of A P Watt Ltd on behalf of The National Trust.

Work for this book was also done at the University of London Library and the British Library, and advice sought from the libraries of the National Army Museum and the Imperial War Museum. Staff at Bateman's, Kipling's former home and now a National Trust property receiving upwards of 60,000 visitors a year, were particularly helpful.

Many thanks are due to Julie Peakman from the Wellcome Trust Centre for her reading and advice on early drafts.

Index